MW00808413

THE INNER WORK PATH

ALSO BY LISA ROMERO FROM INNERWORK BOOKS

Developing the Self
Through the Inner Work Path
in the Light of Anthroposophy

Living Inner Development
The Necessity of True Inner Development
in the Light of Anthroposophy

Sex Education and the Spirit
Understanding Our Communal Responsibility
for the Healthy Development of Gender
and Sexuality within Society

Spirit-led Community
Healing the Impact of Technology

A Bridge to Spirit
Understanding Conscious Self Development
and Consciousness-Altering Substances

The Inner Work Path

A Foundation for Meditative Practice in the Light of Anthroposophy

LISA ROMERO

INNERWORK BOOKS | 2014

2014

INNERWORK BOOKS

PO Box 1064
Mullumbimby NSW 2482
Australia

Copyright © 2014 by Lisa Romero. All rights reserved. No
part of this book may be reproduced, stored in a retrieval
system, or transmitted in any form or by any means,
electronic, mechanical, photocopying, recording, or otherwise
without the written permission of InnerWork Books.

https://www.innerworkpath.com

ISBN: 978-0-6484904-2-5 (paperback)
ISBN: 978-0-6484904-3-2 (eBook)

CONTENTS

Introduction

My intention in putting these pictures into writing is the same as my intention in all my lectures, workshops, and individual work—that they be helpful, that they be useful. This work will not be for everyone, for not all souls are in a place where spiritual activity is consciously central to their lives. If it is central to your life, if you are being called to quicken this development and you are interested in developing capacities rather than satisfying your soul through what it can gain from the bodily nature alone, then this path may be connected to your path. On this path I live honestly with the reality that these exercises and meditations awaken and enhance a deep spiritual life; that they can and do transform human beings. I have experienced this truth in myself and many colleagues of the inner work path.

All human beings are now called upon to do all that we can to help in the evolution and progress of human life. "We are now living in the epoch when it is essential for human beings to be conscious that they must not merely rely upon what flows into them from Cosmic Powers but must themselves cooperate in the Process of world evolution."[1] We are being called to participate in the future of humanity in a new way, and although at times it may feel like an impossible task, we know that we need to keep on trying to achieve it. People are trying in their own ways: many artists strive daily in this quest, for someone else it is through humanitarian work, for others it is in changing policies and law, for some it is educating or bringing up children, and for still others it is through encounters in everyday life. The potential list is endless. We all have a way, even if our task is not clear.

We are not the first beings to develop ourselves for the progress of others, but we are the first beings who are free to not do so. "How would it have been if those Beings who have created what is today outspread in the universe, who bestow so much upon us—how would it have been if they had done nothing in the past to promote their own development? Once, in the infinitely distant past, their forces of thinking, feeling, and willing were just as trivial as our own, and today their power is such that they no longer need to receive strength from the macrocosm; they give, only give."[2]

I met Rudolf Steiner's work when I was twenty years old. My esoteric teacher gave me the book *Knowledge of the Higher Worlds and Its Attainment* to study. I knew nothing of Steiner's other work and its effects on the world. I knew him only as a spiritual teacher. We have been given a wealth of knowledge through this great initiate; knowledge that has had its effects on hundreds of thousands of people through education, medicine, architecture, agriculture, and other fields of endeavor. It was through his spiritual development and capacities that he was able to gain and pass on this knowledge.

In my view, Steiner's ability to herald in this new phase of self-development is his greatest gift. We have a new way of approaching our spiritual life, and to understand this new way is to understand what the world needs now. "Humanity must become a partaker of the spirit in order to carry its revelations into the physical world. Human beings transform the earth by implanting in it what they have ascertained in the spiritual world. That is their task. It is only because the physical world is dependent upon the spiritual, and because human beings can work upon the earth, in a true sense, only if they are participators in those worlds in which the creative forces lie concealed—only for these reasons should they have the desire to ascend to the higher worlds."[3]

This book is a small contribution toward understanding this path of ascending to the higher worlds. Even though it uses terms that may be uncommon to those not familiar with this path, in reading the whole book an understanding of these terms unfolds. The content is dense, and is not intended to be skimmed through, but read and re-read to allow us to work upon it. This allows us to orient, check, and direct ourselves; something that for me is of great use in worlds where the laws are different, and where the terrains are extraordinarily new.

I

STRENGTHENING THE SOUL

How Meditative Practice Works

At the foundation of Western esoteric practices is the deep understanding that human beings are part of the evolution of consciousness. Human beings are here on the earth to bring something new into the evolving spiritual consciousness as well as into physical evolution. Our evolutionary task is to develop freedom and love in the highest sense of the words.

The human being is not only the outer person that we see in front of us; not just the reflection that we perceive in the mirror. It is also, and perhaps more, the inner self that we recognize as our true humanness. It is those inner forces—the capacities that live in our inner life, the capacities of thinking, feeling, and volition—that we recognize as ourselves. When we truly seek to understand where the content of the capacities of thinking, feeling, and willing have arisen, we may find that the aggregate of these three soul forces is not independent of the outer human being that we are and the outer life that we have lived.

Much of who we believe to be our free self has been cultivated through our outer life and has therefore become to a greater or lesser degree dependent upon the outer self. The outer self is the impermanent self. It is the self that must fall away, the self that belongs to earthly life. Many traditions see the physical earthly body as the vehicle for the human soul. The human soul, with its capacities of thinking, feeling, and will activity, is a part of our eternal self. However, it is only those independent capacities, those capacities of the soul that are not dependent on the bodily transient self, which will continue to be a part of our eternal nature. It is in the growth of the eternal soul that we develop—evolve toward love and freedom—yet we are diverted from this evolution through the binding of soul activities to the transient nature of the outer body. In this aspect of the soul we are often the most unloving and the most unfree.

Meditative, contemplative exercises are created and given to develop free soul capacities that are not dependent on the outer self, on our bodily nature. Free soul capacities are developed through exercises that are independent of our past, our conditioning, our biography, and even our constitution, temperament, and gender. These exercises offer us the possibility of waking up to the journey of the evolving soul.

Evolution is taking place for all of humanity. Through meditative exercises we proceed on this journey with greater clarity and speed, for we are not as liable to be waylaid by the forces of the unconscious, the forces of materialism and egotism, and the forces of the great sleep of forgetting who we are and why we are here. It is not that through meditation we will avoid these forces; in fact, meditation will speed up our encounter with and understanding of them. True meditation leads us through the journey that all of humanity will at some point take. We must distinguish the true from the false, the beautiful from the ugly, the good from the malicious; and in the recognition we will find that it is our free will to choose which is our path.

When the human soul is no longer bound to the transient self, it regains its rightful position as a clear mediator between the spiritual world and the physical world. The soul that is satisfied with only what it can gain from its bodily nature can be seen as less evolved. When the soul strives to find its reflection in the spirit, it can be seen as becoming perfected. The more perfected the soul, the greater a servant of the spirit of evolution it is. This may be the only true reason to develop soul capacities—to serve the spirit for the evolution of humanity. The strong soul may cross the threshold consciously into the spiritual world, in which the truth of life is revealed. A soul that is reliant only on its outer nature, the body, is not yet a strong soul; or else it is a strong soul, but has become entangled in the sense world, particularly through the mighty and powerful diverting forces of materialism and egotism.

The Relationship between Body and Soul

There is an intimate relationship between the body and soul; to understand this relationship we must first differentiate the sheaths that make up the external body. We must distinguish the outer human being from the inner human being. The physical body lives in space. It is the body of form. It is what we can experience with our senses. All that is manifest to the external senses has some type of physical body. In its purest form, the mineral kingdom is the archetype of the physical body. In common with the plant kingdom, the human being also has an etheric body. This is our body of life processes, the human being revealed in time. The astral or sentient body, which in various ways is also expressed in the animal kingdom, is another component of the human being. This sentient body allows us to receive sensations, stimulation, and activity through sensory input. It is the foundation for perception of the outer world. These three sheaths make up the outer human being. The outer sheaths have developed over time; the growth of each of these bodies has taken place throughout our entire biography, and by the time we reach adulthood the foundations have been laid. The inner human being, the soul and the ego or I-consciousness, which belong to no other kingdom that is perceptible other than our human kingdom, unites with and relies upon these foundations in everyday life.[4]

The inner human soul has three aspects—the sentient soul, the intellectual or mind soul, and the consciousness soul. The sentient soul unites with the sentient body, the intellectual soul unites with the etheric body, and the consciousness soul unites with the physical body. As the outer body grows up, the soul grows down, until they are intimately and necessarily bound. Our everyday consciousness, our waking day-consciousness, arises from our ego, I-consciousness, and this relationship of the intimately bound body and soul.

The human being gathers the greater forces needed to maintain a continuation of consciousness outside the sense world through liberating the soul from its dependence on the outer self, and by transforming what has been bestowed upon us in the form of the three bodily sheaths. Human evolution required the knitting together of body and soul. Otherwise, we would not gain the strength that builds from freeing ourselves. We would not experience our separated, individualized life, which develops these capacities and allows the continuation of consciousness in the ocean of spiritual existence.

Understanding these three soul activities is essential to understanding the path of the inner work. The first, known as the sentient soul, functions in our inner life in several ways. The most commonly understood is its capacity to register pleasure and pain, and to seek pleasure and avoid pain. If we tickle the inside of our arms, the sentient body transmits the sensation, but it is the sentient soul that likes or dislikes the sensation. Everyone does not have the same response; some enjoy being tickled on the inside of the arm, and for others it is irritating. All the sensations we experience through our development are registered as liking or disliking, wanting or not wanting.

The sentient soul is also responsible for how we make associations inwardly. It is the ground on which we make these connections. When in conversation with another we do not stay completely present to the conversation, but are constantly connecting present thoughts and images with our past conscious and unconscious experiences; this is the sentient soul at work in its relationship to what is stored in the sentient body. For example, if a friend talks of a trip he has taken overseas, it is common to unconsciously associate your own images with the other's experience. These images sometimes link directly, and sometimes indirectly, to what the other is saying. For example, he may be talking about a recent trip to Italy, and you think about a pair of shoes. Why think of a pair of shoes? Even though you may no longer be conscious of it, it could be because another friend had spoken to you about expensive Italian shoes. If you stop to ponder why you had the thought about shoes, you may find the association from your past experience. In such a moment, it is the sentient soul that makes the connection.

We make sentient soul connections far more often than we might imagine. When it is unconsciously at work, the sentient soul relies upon the sentient body for its information. This means that the sentient soul, when it is in an unconscious relationship to the sentient body, relies on past experience; all that has been inscribed in our development up until this moment becomes the basis for the sentient soul's knowledge. For example, you may meet a person with whom you immediately feel uncomfortable. You do not trust the person, and you assume it is something that lives in the other person. However, that individual may be wearing the same color clothing that your tyrannical schoolteacher used to wear. The sentient soul makes this association via its relationship with the inscribed sentient body; and it does not allow you to meet this individual. Instead, in such cases, we meet the past, and with this past we often meet our "unfreedom."

We bring our past, especially our painful past, into our everyday experiences. Consider a person who has had a childhood experience of being excluded and carries the experience into adulthood because it is inscribed into his sentient body. Why an event is inscribed into one person's sentient body but not into another's belongs to the deeper mysteries. Many individuals experience exclusion, and it is in our interest to understand the purpose of some of these common human experiences.

In adult life we continue to carry all our inscribed experiences unconsciously within us until they are transformed. If the experience of being excluded is carried within us, the present life is veiled by it. Let us say, for example, that a teacher who carries a childhood experience of exclusion comes upon three colleagues talking together. As the teacher approaches, the three colleagues stop talking and look down at the ground. From the teacher's point of view, exclusion has occurred again. The old emotions, the old feelings of rejection, rise up again. This response is more often than not an error in judging the situation. What actually just took place may have been quite different. Perhaps it happened like this: one of the colleagues noticed a strange insect on the ground and pointed it out to the others. They stopped talking together and looked down at the ground, fixing their attention on the insect.

We often do not read life as it is, but instead through the veils of our own past experience, which we carry within us. In that moment the soul, being body-bound, is not free. It could be stated that all soul activity that is body-bound is unfree, even when it is not in error. When the sentient soul is bound to the sentient body, it is functioning from the past and is unable to be alert, present, and in a state of new learning to meet the present moment. Can the soul meet life as it is, as life wishes to speak and be seen? It is here that we understand the wisdom from the esoteric path: "Before the eyes can see, they must be incapable of tears. Before the ear can hear, it must have lost its sensitiveness."[5] Body-bound, the soul is affected in its thinking, feeling, and actions by the past; although it may be unaware of this, it is not present to the now.

The intellectual or mind soul also functions in several ways. One way is by inwardly connecting sequences of images or thoughts. In a healthy person, this sequencing has a logical form. One thought logically comes after the next. When we follow a train of thinking, we can also connect the thoughts through a feeling for the truth of the ideas. When we listen to someone speaking, even if it is on an unfamiliar subject, we can still experience a recognition of the truth behind what is said. We listen behind the words to hear the speaker's meaning. This recognition has a quality of feeling about it. We do not have to know if it is right, but we feel the rightness of it. It resonates with us. This may also be expressed as understanding the meaning of the other, following and understanding the concepts.

This is one way the intellectual soul functions in our inner life.

Through its binding with the sentient body, the sentient soul associates different images and thoughts that are connected to the content of what is perceived. Likewise, at a deeper level of the soul's activity, we have conditioned ways of thinking, what may be called beliefs. These are beliefs that have been constructed so that we no longer need to think through one thought after the other individually, consecutively, freely; rather we jump in our thinking to meaning that has already been developed. When the intellectual soul is body-bound— bound to the etheric body that has been inscribed upon by our culture, our religion, our family, and our society throughout our development—we make personal associations through what we perceive from the outer world, and also judgments, conclusions, and assumptions, based on what already lives in us.

Our beliefs are often conditionings. When we penetrate them, they may not be our personal intentions at all; we may not consciously agree with them even though we live by them. It is very difficult to penetrate these beliefs because we do not even know that we have them. They live below the threshold of consciousness in such a way that they influence our decisions, our judgments, and our behaviors without our awareness.

Unfortunately, many beliefs that we carry are not in alignment with the truth. They do not reflect the wisdom of the spirit. They do not reflect the eternal, and invariably they limit our relationship with the world and therefore restrict our growth in the world. Many beliefs are such that we assume them to be right, and that others must also share the same beliefs if they are to be right, and not wrong. Atheists, for example, through their view of the world, cannot understand how religion can exist because they do not have a feeling for religion that religious believers have. Atheists have factual, logical thought based on what can be perceived by the physical senses, and that is their belief.

When the etheric body is greatly imbalanced, the thought structures of a person do not make sense in the context of society's norms. These imbalanced forms are passed on to the intellectual soul. If this imbalance is strong, we call it a mental disorder. Mental disorders can be seen as thought sequences that do not make sense in the sense world, and in terms of the constructs that society has agreed upon. However, we do accept certain differences, such as those between an atheist and a believer in God—even though each may think that the other is delusional, undeveloped, and disconnected from the truth.

We all have errors in our thinking patterns. We do not know that we have errors because these patterns do not reveal themselves to our everyday consciousness. They have been bestowed upon us by our family life, our religion, our culture and society. In our community of life with others, sometimes these errors are revealed to us. Community can sometimes help us to see and transform the etheric patterns laid down in childhood. Experiencing other cultures can help us see ourselves. Being immersed in a different culture can reveal to us the etheric habits that affect our behavior. In Japan, for example, no Japanese person would question whether a taxi driver was taking a longer route to a destination in order to earn more money. It would not enter the passenger's thinking. It is a nearly impossible thought for the Japanese. The cultural norm prevails. In Australia, on the other hand, an Australian would look out to make sure that a taxi driver is taking the quickest route. This does not mean that Australian taxi drivers are deceitful, but that in Australian culture people would ask the question.

We rely on patterns of thinking without any conscious awareness of it. When we search our thinking, we will see that we are all influenced by such patterns and beliefs. We live with these patterns and are oblivious to them; if we are not oblivious to them we are often lazy in regard to them. For instance, a woman says, "I want to overcome my abandonment issue. It's causing me difficulty." She continues, "I was speaking to my husband, and he said he was at the office. When I put the phone down, a colored man came to my door. I locked the door and shouted to him to get off my property. I called my husband back, because he would want to know. He was not there, and his secretary said he had not been there for a couple of hours. I was beside myself because I have been betrayed before. When he got home, he explained that he was at the other office, and I realized it was all my stuff." The woman sees her abandonment issue because it causes her pain in the present situation, even though it is her past at work through her sentient soul. But she does not see her prejudice against other cultures and people of other colors; this is her past via her intellectual soul. She just lives with it and does not even recognize it as a problem, does not question it, and certainly does not attempt to resolve it. Daily we live out of patterns that are not the truth. Not only are we unfree; but we also are often in error in our unfreedom. We see that all distinctions made by unconsciously judging human beings according to race, gender, age, or social position are, in fact, errors that have been passed on to us and that we live with and act from, even if we consciously do not agree with them.

The consciousness soul is the deepest activity of all, for through it we experience our sense of self. It reflects our personal, individualized will. Until we have developed the capacity to have soul activity that is not bound to the body, the consciousness soul finds its identity as a separate entity through the physical body. "This is who I am, I am such and such"; it is a necessary experience of the earthly life. In our need to preserve and maintain this sense of self, we may even defend this identity. Often it becomes the greatest ground for disharmony with another human being; we want to prevail both physically and in our identity as we know ourselves.

The consciousness soul, if reflected from harmonious body activity, will appear as an identity that is strong and intact. If, however, this body activity is deeply imbalanced, it can affect the sense of a healthy identity. Taken to the extreme, it also causes such disorders as paranoia or megalomania. If the soul is dependent on the body to mirror harmony and the mirror is cracked, then the soul is reflected back in a distorted manner.

If the consciousness soul, independent of the physical body, has a strong "I" sense, a strong individualized sense of self, it can overcome the errors that live in the bodily sheaths because it does not require the bodily sheaths to produce its sense of self. In this way the errors of the past may still be present and untransformed, but the effects no longer have an impact on the present moment. The strongest one wins out! If the outer human being is dominant in force, it wins, and its pattern is reflected to the inner soul activity.

When we observe young children, we see that their inner stability is greatly affected by their bodily wellbeing. It is the necessity of childhood that the body and soul become united. From the tenth year the child may become aware of the distinction between self and body, but it is not until around the age of sixteen that the soul can potentially begin to form its independence from the bodily nature. It is not until adulthood that we can consciously direct our soul activity away from the outer self. It is then that we can begin the liberation of the inner human being from the outer human being. This we must do for ourselves. Rudolf Steiner said that either the outer self or the inner self has the upper hand. Which has the upper hand? It is always the strongest one. The strongest one wins out! In this light, Steiner recasts Plato's famous allegory to "Be the chariot rider and not the horse." If my bodily nature is stronger, my soul, my inner life, will be affected by the past. It will be affected by all that lives in me. As we meet life at various moments, we can experience which is stronger—the body and its effects on the soul or the independent, free soul activity. Freeing the soul means standing in and relating to the moment, learning in the present.

The Inner Work

The untrained soul is used to being bound to the body. When we stop our activity of freely working inwardly with our thought life, it returns to its original bodily connection. No one can prevent this without continuous effort, unless several stages of awakening have been achieved. The soul returns to its default position as if on autopilot. The exercises are like weights; in lifting them, we build muscles in the soul so that it may be independent of bodily activity. Like muscle development, it takes time, energy, and attention. Time, energy, and attention are like the soil, the sun, and the rain to our inner life. Whatever you feed, grows. Rather than place our time, energy, and attention on all the errors of our soul, our past conditionings, and the traumas and experiences of childhood, we acknowledge the error or pattern but work energetically toward building what can truly free us—liberated independent soul activity. It is through this liberated soul activity that we can become a student of life, opening up and learning what life teaches us.

As St. Teresa of Ávila put it in the poem "Feeling Desperate":

The
earth
and sky will open their purse for you
and your life will
change
if with all your heart you say these words each day,
"Teach me, dear God, all that you
know."

One night I walked through the streets
feeling desperate, in need of
alchemy.

A hooded priest passed by where there were no lamps.
I could not see his face, I only heard these words that he
kept repeating,

"Teach me, dear Lord, all that you know."

I knew a treasure had
entered my
soul.[6]

Distinguishing the true from the false, the beautiful from the ugly, and the good from the immoral in itself awakens us; but we then need to turn to the path that connects us with the divine, or at least to the path toward the higher self. This is where the exercises are the most helpful. They are not trying to make our lives easier, or our personalities prettier, or change the way others act toward us. Giving time, energy, and attention to the error feeds the error. Therefore our everyday self, which is often overly identified with our outer being and its errors, does not find its fulfillment in esoteric exercises.

It is always strengthening to the inner being to recognize that it is caught in the outer self; that it has become the horse again and must work toward being the chariot rider through the work of turning the soul toward the liberated soul, and then toward the divine. The path is hard work. As Steiner said, "The esoteric path is either difficult, or it is no path at all."[7] Yet life grows richer for this striving. The strong soul experiences the depth of life, the wonder of life, and the evolution of life in a way that is impossible through the unconsciousness of our body-bound existence.

The gift of our body-bound existence is that it shows us where we are still attached and unfree. The biography is the incarnating soul's work to transform in this lifetime. When we feel justified in taking certain positions and making certain judgments, or when we blame another for certain feelings we have, we see where we are attached. The esoteric student begins to understand and appreciate these words of initiation, "If anyone can make you feel anything, you are still not free." The student recognizes that personal feelings lead us to greater self-awareness and responsibility. But this work is not comfortable for an attached soul, which is, to begin with, reluctant to take on such responsibility. When the soul is able to stand in life in this new way, it becomes a student of life. Then we become keen students of the life that is expressing itself in and through our own biography.

In the words of St. John of the Cross from the poem "Development":

Once I said to God, "How do you teach us?"

And He replied,

"If
you were
playing chess with someone who
had infinite power and infinite knowledge
and wanted to make you a
master of the
game,

where would all the chess
pieces be at every
moment?"

Indeed, not only where he wanted them,
but where all were best for your
development;

and that is every situation
of one's
life."[8]

Each of the exercises given in esoteric work has the purpose of strengthening the inner human being. To understand each exercise and how they affect various soul activities is extremely important because the soul needs not simply to strengthen but also to do so in a harmonized way, balanced in its capacities of thinking, feeling, and willing.

All genuine spiritual schooling is founded on four pillars. The first is the ability to distinguish the transient from the non-transient in the world. The second is to seek for the eternal being in ourselves. The third is cultivation of the six virtues (which the six subsidiary exercises are only the preparation for). The fourth is the love of liberation, the love of freedom.

Steiner gives what are commonly called "six subsidiary exercises" as a way to develop and purify the thinking, feeling, and willing. The concentration exercise is one of the six subsidiary or hygienic exercises that is working toward the development of one of the six virtues. The concentration exercise asks us to focus on a simple man-made object, such as a pin or a pencil, and attempt to imagine this object in our mind's eye. From this point, we build a logical sequence of thoughts that relates to this object. What is the size of the object, what materials are used in making the object, how would these materials be gathered, and so on. It is not important that we know the answer to these questions. What is important is to actively engage inwardly in forming and building the questions in a logical sequence.[9]

As simple as this exercise appears, it works on strengthening the sentient soul through the image that we hold in our mind's eye. The very thought of the object strengthens the sentient soul because we create it independently of anything unconsciously arising within the soul's activity. We choose to will this exercise. We do not pick an object each day that randomly pops into our heads, but rather choose the object we want to work with. We consciously participate in our thinking, not just in associating from the past or with lazy thinking. It is generally most easy to experience the activity of the sentient soul, the image or the thought. To experience the intellectual soul, we have to experience the activity that takes place before forming the image—what creates the image. It is to experience, not the thought but instead the sequence of thoughts, the streaming of soul activity.

The sequencing of thoughts strengthens the intellectual soul. This is not a memory exercise that runs through the mind daily. Instead, we must awaken to the sequence of logical thoughts connected with the object we have chosen. The will to do so arises from the consciousness soul. To truly distinguish among the three soul activities during the concentration exercise, we can place our attention more strongly on each one separately. In the beginning, it is difficult to distinguish all three soul processes clearly; it is almost impossible to witness clearly each of the soul activities separately and simultaneously in the same moment. However, we can experience for ourselves these three activities.

If we try this concentration exercise we will notice that there are three distinct activities of the soul. Some people can experience these activities spatially. The image of the object, the thought of the object, is usually in front of the forehead. Most students experience that the images are found here. The sequence of thoughts can be experienced spatially around the middle of the head, streaming toward the image. The willing that is behind the sequencing of thoughts and that strengthens the consciousness soul is often experienced spatially at the back of the head.

To more distinctly experience the three separate soul activities, we need to eliminate what we have built up. When we take away or extinguish the image and experience only the activity that creates the image, the activity that streams toward the image, we begin to experience the workings of the intellectual soul more distinctly. When we remove the activity, what is left is the will behind the streaming; then we will begin to experience the consciousness soul more clearly.

When the image and the streaming are removed, some people say that what is left is the self. The reason is that the ego, the "I," lights up most actively in the consciousness soul. It also lights up in the intellectual soul, but not as clearly. Least of all does it light up in the sentient soul. Through our free soul activity the "I" is experienced with greater clarity. Without free soul activity, the "I" itself is body-bound and egotism takes over, or the lower I-experience is the result. Through our free soul activity, the "I" in its higher nature can be active—its true nature is revealed. What are the signs of the true nature of the "I"? The ego lights up most clearly in the consciousness soul. It first expresses itself through this same soul capacity. If the true "I" is our spiritual nature, then this true "I" is love, as the spirit is love. The Indian poet Rabindranath Tagore said: "When all the strings of my life will be tuned, my Master, then at every touch of thine will come out the music of love."[10]

The spirit uses the vehicle of the soul to express itself. Love is expressed through the consciousness soul's ground of activity, through the will, through the deed. The first sign of the human being's awakening to the true "I" is the expression of love. This is love as a deed in the world—not as a feeling for another, but first as a willingness to help. This willingness can be expressed in various ways. One is as empathy. True empathy is the ability to unite with others' suffering, to put ourselves in their shoes. True empathy has the consciousness soul quality of becoming one with the other.

The meditations we are working with on this well-trodden path have been given by initiates who have developed the soul capacity to bring from the spiritual world these meditation exercises. These meditations come from the eternal, from the truth that is traced out in the spiritual world. They are not arbitrary exercises made up because they are interesting or affect soul function. They have a specific purpose, each one developing various soul capacities. Some exercises may be seen as universal, and therefore may be utilized by many souls. They contain within them the archetypes of soul development. If we take a look at two of the verses that Steiner gave frequently in early esoteric classes perhaps we can perceive this.

(1)

More radiant than the sun,
Purer than the snow,
Finer than the ether
Is the Self,
The Spirit in my heart of hearts.
I am this Self.
This Self am I.

(2)

In purest outpoured light
Shimmers the Godhead of the world.
In purest Love toward all that is
Outpours the godhood of my soul.
I rest within the Godhead of the world;
There shall I find myself,
Within the Godhead of the world.[11]

In these verses, whose origin is in the Bhagavad Gita, we may perceive what is strengthened here. The soul is given its direction away from the bodily nature. The true "I" is more than what is perceptible to us in ordinary earthly life. We are given images, thoughts that lead the soul in the direction of the spirit. We are given a picture of where we may find the true "I." It is the soul's journey to turn toward the spirit, to receive from the spirit, and then to give back to the world. The image in the verse, worked upon, strengthens the sentient soul. The sequence of thoughts guides us and strengthens the intellectual soul. The willing activity that we give to the verse, to be immersed in it with our thinking, our feeling, and our will, strengthens the consciousness soul. As with the concentration exercise, all three soul activities are strengthened.

It is important to recognize that these spiritual verses give us more than a weight to pull upon; they give us food from the eternal. In them are contained imaginations from the spirit world. Imaginations are also expressions of spiritual deeds that have been, that are, and that will become. Through imaginations we can perceive the spiritual reality behind the world of appearance, the external world. The verses also contain spiritual activity, powers that are inspirations. In them, beings of evolution and the Masters of Wisdom and Harmony are at work. Each meditative exercise calls us into relationship with the spiritual world. The more we give ourselves to the exercises, the more we immerse ourselves in the world of spiritual consciousness.

These gifts do more than strengthen our soul; they form us, as the child is formed in the womb of the mother, developing the organs that enable perception of the outer world after birth. We begin developing organs that enable us to perceive the spiritual world when we are born anew, individualized on a higher plane of consciousness. Only the free components of the soul are fashioned into organs of perception of spiritual activity. Initially, it is the free sentient soul that becomes the organ for perceiving imagination; the free intellectual soul that receives inspiration; and the free consciousness soul that is the ground of intuition. Through these three soul capacities we perceive the thoughts of spiritual beings, we experience the activity of spiritual beings, and we unite with the consciousness of spiritual beings.

The Gifts

There are numerous exercises, verses, meditations, imaginations, and mantras gifted to us in esoteric training—each one having its effect on developing the soul and guiding us into a conscious relationship with the spiritual world. These exercises can be categorized most simply by the three primary spiritual capacities that they develop: imagination, inspiration, and intuition.

The first is imagination or image-consciousness. The human being has an unconscious or semiconscious image-consciousness already. The human being's innate unconscious or semiconscious imagination is evident in our ability to associate, to dream, to experience pictures arising in thought. The free soul develops conscious image-consciousness. This will allow us to see into the realm of imagination, where the pictures arise. To have an insight into the laws of the world of imagination, we can consider dreaming consciousness; what we do at night between deep sleep and waking day-consciousness. It is clear that we affect our dreams by things that we have seen in the day and associations that we have made—these thoughts and feelings are transformed into images. Those who view their dreams will recognize the jumbled, unclear nature of them and understand that the laws of earthly life do not belong to the dream world. We can be standing in one country one moment, and seconds later be on the other side of the world. The image of a friend can turn into the image of a monster. We can fly. We can dream an epic dream that goes on seemingly for hours, and yet only five minutes will have passed on the earthly clock. If I fear something in the dream, it may change its appearance into something more fearful. If I love something, it may change its appearance to something more loving. Much of our everyday, workaday self mingles with this image world. For the student of the inner work the world of image-consciousness must be free from all subjectivity, or what we receive in our inner life will not come from the spiritual world but from our personal world.

Putting one's self to one side, extinguishing the subjective self, is at first impossible for the soul that is bound to the body. The soul that has not developed independent strength and activity will fear losing itself, will fear annihilation, and through this kind of self-love will cling more tightly to what it knows itself to be—the outer human being.

We love ourselves more than anything else in the world—this self-love must have been overcome if we are to be able to shut ourselves out of our consciousness. We must, in actual fact, come to the point where we say to ourselves: As I am now, I must eliminate myself.... I must put myself to one side; for if I do not shut out completely all those things in me that otherwise I quite like to feel in myself: errors, trivialities, prejudices, sympathies, antipathies—if I do not put these right away then my ascent into the higher worlds cannot be made aright.[12]

We cannot carry our subjective self and its effects in our soul into our relationship to the spiritual world and its various planes of consciousness if we wish to perceive the truth of what is there.

In order to learn how to put our self to one side, how to extinguish the sentient soul, we have to first work to build an imaginative picture out of our very own soul forces. We build this imaginative picture not from association or from memory but from our free inner effort. When we consciously use our soul forces in this manner, we use the forces that originally were bestowed upon us from the spiritual world—the same substance that connects us with what livingly exists as spiritual imagination. When our soul, with effort, works consciously to imagine, it works out of the same realm and in the same realm in which imagination is experienced. The soul is not only a citizen of the earthly world, it is also a citizen of the soul world.[13] Now with the sense world set aside, the soul's primary activity flows directly from the soul itself; it therefore enters this very same world inwardly. The soul world is not an external world in the same sense as the physical world. It is a realm of consciousness.

The imagination exercises strengthen the soul and become a doorway to the world of soul. To enter into relationship with this world consciously, we must eliminate the imagination completely. There is a general rule; we can only fully eliminate what we ourselves have created out of our own free soul activity. If we do not eliminate what we ourselves have created, we will not have the capacity to receive the imagination that streams toward us from the spiritual world. The student of the esoteric path must become accustomed to eliminating the self before receiving spiritual imaginations. Much preparation and purification of the soul are required before it has the strength to think, feel, and will independently of the outer self. This preparation allows the soul to speak, as it were, out of itself, but empty of its own content, receiving what wishes to speak back.

Eliminating our soul content requires great strength, because we are used to filling ourselves inwardly. Even though through these exercises, we gain a new conscious fullness, an active and attentive fullness, we still find it difficult to take the next step of surrendering ourselves in devotion to the other. Only those who know that they can eliminate themselves can trust the imaginations that are given to the inner life.

Developing the capacity to receive inspirations requires another level of training. To have insight into this activity, we can think about deep sleep consciousness. In deep sleep we are no longer dreaming. The majority of people recognize that they have missed deep sleep only when they lack the forces, the energy, the vitality that deep sleep provides. What is happening spiritually in deep sleep? The image world has been set aside, but something still takes place; it is activity without image. Before the image is made manifest, the creative activity that causes it to manifest is present.

During the night, in deep sleep, we receive powers that fortify us. Each morning, when we wake to meet the day, it is through these powers and forces that we have received during our deep sleep that we feel refreshed. But the powers we have for the day are not the same each morning. Some mornings we are full of strength, and other mornings we may feel inwardly peaceful. We gather various forces in deep sleep; it is as though we have been gifted with powers to do the work of our waking day.

We receive spiritual imaginations, and through this power we also receive fructifying forces from the spiritual world and its inhabitants. The meditative exercises prepare us to receive conscious inspirations in a way that is different from soul imaginations. A purely imaginative exercise would have us hold an image. The inspirational aspect of the exercise is the sequencing of thoughts and of images; what is left, after taking away or extinguishing the individual image, the individual thought, and seeking the power behind the thought is the activity being expressed—the activity that allows the image to be built up. The inspirational aspect of the exercise are the forces, the powers that create the image. The power behind the color red is different from the power behind the color blue. The inspirational aspect of an exercise is also experienced in the feeling power that is activated while entering into the exercise. An exercise that is primarily inspirational focuses on the experience and not on the image.

An example of a primarily inspirational exercise is this: imagine the rising sun, experiencing this picture as though the rising sun is an activity within. Then imagine the moonrise, and experience the difference in becoming the moonrise. The focus is on the experience of feeling that arises with the two polarities of sunrise and moonrise.

In the Rose Cross meditation, which is explained in the following chapter, we build an image of a black wooden cross and seven red roses arranged in a circle around the cross's intersection point. The image itself is the imagination part of the meditation, and the building of the image and the feeling that we hold while building it comprise the inspirational aspect of the meditation. The inspirational aspect of the meditation is amplified when we extinguish the image; what is left is the activity that created the image, the activity that streams from weaving the image. All that we needed to do in order to bring the image to consciousness remains after the image has been extinguished.

To receive spiritual inspirations, we must use those same activity forces; we must be active in our sequencing of thought and active in our feeling, pouring ourselves forward. Then we must be able to extinguish all this. We have built up a picture of an image. It is required as an activity, but we must first extinguish the image and become aware of the activity that lives behind it. To receive spiritual inspirations, we must also extinguish the activity; only then may we experience what resounds from the spiritual world in response to our own free soul activity that we have given to the exercise.

In meditative practice, this is a deep place; all that is left is emptiness, empty consciousness. We may experience the vastness of consciousness, but there is no activity, no thought, no image, no weaving, no surging. If something enters into this emptiness, it enters from the spirit. Meditators are clear that it does not come from themselves. They know for certain that their own personal soul activity has been extinguished, because they also know when it stirs within. They know it intimately, as they have abided in the stillness.

Intuition is the next faculty that is developed. When we say in everyday life, "I had an intuition that you were going to call," it is not an intuition in the esoteric sense of the word. Such feelings are more like imaginations. A thought or image of something unknown to the conscious mind has expressed itself. In the esoteric use of the word, intuition is uniting the self with the other. There is no division. There is continual "I" awareness, and yet no separation from the other with which the consciousness unites. To completely understand this, we would have to investigate death consciousness, which is not possible in our everyday experience.

Through development in meditation, we cultivate the possibility of experiencing "conscious universal consciousness." This is "to die before we die," as the Sufis say. It is an experience that becomes possible in meditation after we have extinguished all that we have activated out of our own soul forces, when we are left with empty consciousness. Another step of surrender is required here. It is the hardest surrender of all.

In empty consciousness the consciousness soul stands alone. The consciousness soul, the will being, has been strengthened through meditative exercises. It is strengthened through the rhythm of the mantra. It is strengthened by the will force that is placed into each exercise. It is strengthened by any intuition exercise that involves uniting ourselves with the other so that there is no separation. The human being becomes one with the other being. Yet it is most strongly strengthened through the extinguishing of the other soul forces. It is strengthened by standing alone. It is only from this place of aloneness that it can become All.

Most meditative exercises given in the mystery schools involve all three soul forces. These meditations strengthen the independent sentient soul, intellectual soul, and consciousness soul forces if they are worked correctly. Certain exercises have a definite emphasis on one or another aspect of soul development. These would be given to ensure that a balance of thinking, feeling, and willing is developed. Thinking, feeling, and willing live in all three soul sheaths. In the sentient soul, thought is dominant; in the intellectual soul, feeling is central; and in the consciousness soul, the will predominates. These three need to be equally unfolded and developed in the three soul sheaths. The so-called personal meditations are given to harmonize one-sided soul development. The teacher who understands these exercises intimately is able to perceive with clarity the student's individual need and may personalize the universal practice.

Many traditional meditation methods in mainstream teachings concentrate primarily on accessing the consciousness soul by working with empty consciousness, extinguishing the self, and seeing all else as illusion, as maya. These methods can also utilize breathing exercises, body awareness, and particular postures, and they employ various techniques that enhance letting go of thinking and feeling.

It is possible to develop more fully only one soul capacity and still cross the threshold into the spiritual world. Each capacity separates from the others and works independently in the spiritual world. But this leads to only part of the picture, part of the expression that humanity needs to acquire in order to fulfill its task. If we do not know this, if we are unprepared, then experiencing only part of the truth (which at the time feels like the whole truth) can lead an individual to choose a path of self-development over a path of world development, which ultimately leads to the downfall of that individual. Each of the three distinguishable soul activities enables us to have a different relationship with the spiritual world.

To live in life connected with humanity's evolution, we require the capacity to experience the spirit's direction in its worldly expression. If we are to be conscious participants in humanity's evolution, we need to awaken the faculties of imagination and inspiration as well as intuition. To be in service to others, the soul needs to bridge the spiritual life and the outer life. For this work, all three of the soul capacities are required.

We are citizens of three worlds. In our earthly life we are citizens of the sense world, the soul world, and the spiritual world. When we leave behind the sense world and penetrate our inner life, we feel more strongly our citizenship in the soul world and the spiritual world. When we leave behind the soul world, we are truly citizens of the spiritual world. The soul is the bridge between the heavens and the earth. The spiritual world would be completely veiled from us if the soul's forces, like silk threads woven together and placed upon the invisible spiritual self, were not there to bring the spirit to life for us. The soul forces that emulate the spiritual world become these silk threads. They are a part of the eternal.

The eternal self is all that which has been freed from the transient world. The human soul participates in this transient world; when uniting with it, for as much as it does unite, it becomes bound to the transient. It is these soul forces that need to be transformed after death, released again from their binding. The human soul that participates consciously in the spiritual world participates only as much as it is free. When we strive to live out of the eternal in us, we strive to live out of the eternal in the world. We avoid acting out of our personal will. We seek to act from the higher will, knowing that the personal will leads us to more binding and that the spiritual self is working on behalf of the evolving spirit of the world. This soul development allows us to cross the threshold into the spiritual world.

The first universal consciousness soul crossing is a life-changing experience, for we know the truth of who we are. We know for certain that we do not die. Each crossing reveals life-changing truth, truth that sets us free. It must be lived individually by those who walk the path. It is not a truth that can be passed on from one individual to the other. Thomas Aquinas stated the esoteric reality, "Every truth, no matter who speaks it, comes from God." We can recognize this truth in ourselves, even if we have not experienced it. If we have experienced it, we *know* it to be the truth.

How these threshold crossings will live in us afterward depends on the preparation the soul makes before the crossing. Let us not forget the maxim that every person resembles the god he or she understands. The possibility is that if this crossing occurs without certain preparations about the wisdom of the evolution of humanity, then the experience may leave us feeling that there is no point to life. This experience may pull us out of our relationship to the world. This holds true for all spiritual insight arising in this particular realm of the spiritual world. Each spiritual crossing is but a stepping stone on this great path. Without preparation, we may find ourselves wanting to get off the wheel of life and death, to leave behind this evolution of humanity because we do not recognize it as such.

What we receive as inspiration and as imagination from the spiritual world imparts these pictures of human evolution. We feel united with the human task to develop freedom and, in the truest sense, to develop love. These imaginations have passed down through the mystery schools. They keep us connected to the whole of humanity, to humanity's journey. The beings that inspire us from the spiritual world give power to these imaginations, and therein they continue to live. They may feed us, sustain us. They give to us what we need to continue the great work. The human being prepared in this way is not pulled away from human progress but rather unites more deeply with it, unites with humanity's evolution. This is a significant point for the modern initiate and the present-day neophyte. For they are called to bear the progression of the human soul that carves the path that all humanity will walk. Personal shortcuts are forsaken for the collective journey.

The occultist must walk this path to make the way clearer and more defined for those a step or more behind. The great initiates bring in the next step and the new direction of the evolving human consciousness. It is clear that anthroposophy, through the great initiate Rudolf Steiner, heralds the new development of conscious image-consciousness. This is a main component of development for the present collective path. It is the next step that must awaken for all, even though individually a person may be working beyond this step. Our progression in the spiritual world always requires consciousness soul development to be fully active at the level we have achieved. Even so, we must not forsake the collective path.

The inner path, the path of initiation, is not singled out for a few individuals. The whole of humanity is being called to the task. The schools of initiation and esoteric training are there to support humanity so that it will not be waylaid or diverted on the journey. It is possible for self-initiation to occur; if individuals are capable of great attention and great devotion, then life itself will initiate them. It is likely, however, that such individuals—those able in this incarnation to awaken to the schooling of life itself—went through the preparation of initiation schooling in previous incarnations.

PREPARATION THROUGH PRACTICE

The foundational meditative practice has a universal form. Each component has a reason and a purpose. This traditional form schools the soul in several ways. It consists of four primary components: restfulness of soul; the verse or direction; the main exercise, which is exercising for soul strength; and the extinguishing of soul activities. First, we begin our practice with a "restfulness of soul" exercise. Its purpose is to put our everyday self, the "me" self, to one side. We put it to one side so that we can engage our soul forces separately from our everyday self. If we omit this starting exercise, we often find that after the verse, or the main exercise, all that we have achieved is restfulness of soul. It is useful, but this is not the purpose of the exercises that have a far greater service for us than separating ourselves from our everyday self. We need to begin all meditative work from a place of restfulness. Experienced meditators come to this restfulness very quickly because the soul is used to stepping out of everyday thinking, feeling, and willing. Most others need training to begin with. Each exercise has a purpose; in this case it is to begin separating our soul's inner life from our outer life.

Three rest exercises are given here, each working on a soul to help it release from daily binding to the outer life of thinking, feeling, and willing. These exercises are very different to experience; although thinking, feeling, and willing are intimately connected in everyday life, they are not necessarily equally active. We may require only one exercise to put ourselves to one side, to experience rest-fulness of soul. We may, however, require more than one exercise to ready ourselves for meditative practice.

EXERCISE I

Unbinding the Thinking: "Is This I?"

This simple exercise helps us put ourselves to one side. It is especially useful if the thinking is overly bound to our everyday consciousness. Steiner suggested that we regularly view ourselves as though we are sitting on a mountaintop looking down upon our lives. This exercise removes from us our tendency to overly identify with the "me" self.

Sitting comfortably in a chair, generally with the eyes closed, we begin to observe ourselves. Anything that is distracting us is questioned by focusing our attention on it and then asking the question—not answering, simply asking—"Is this I?" Examples: We experience the pressure of the chair against the body. "Is this I?" We hear the sounds around us. "Is this I?" We observe the rising and falling of the breath. "Is this I?" We feel the sensations in the body. "Is this I?" We review the thoughts in the mind. "Is this I?" And so on. We observe whatever is catching us, look at it, and ask, "Is this I?" (From the realm of the spiritual world all is "I," but in our everyday, "me" self we must first become the observer. We must begin from where our consciousness is in the present moment.) This simple exercise can bring restfulness of soul for those whose thinking is attached to the outer world.

EXERCISE 2

Unbinding the Feeling: "Rest"

The rest exercise is useful particularly when the feeling life is overly bound. Steiner used the word *Ruhe*, a German word that refers, not to a period of rest between activities, but rather to a state of being. The word *rest* in English does not suffice; the quality of restfulness, peacefulness, or something similar may be more apropos. Sitting comfortably in a chair, generally with the eyes closed, we allow ourselves to become the word *rest*. We drink in this quality of being. Holding the word in our consciousness alone is not the exercise. Living the word is what is asked of us. We do not do this by the clock but until we feel we are no longer meshed in our everyday cares and worries.

EXERCISE 3

Unbinding the Will: "Smiling"

A smile is the balance between laughter and frowning. It produces health-giving effects. When a teacher smiles at a student, it effects change for the student. This exercise supports the quality of rest, not relaxation, in the body. It is not a preparation for sleep but rather an enlivening rest. When we smile, it is both an opening and an awakening, an activity full of rest.

We begin by sitting comfortably in a chair, generally with the eyes closed. Start by actually smiling, in case we have forgotten how; retain this quality. Then, placing our attention upon our feet, we imagine that the feet smile. It is a feeling of both rest and activity in the feet. We then move to the ankles, and the ankles smile. Then we progress to the calves, and we help the calves to smile. We move on to the knees, and the knees smile (there is often resistance in the knees). Now move up the legs until the legs are smiling. Continue to the buttocks and pelvic regions and help them smile. Then the lower abdomen and the lower back smile. Slowly, we travel through the body, smiling. We become aware of any place that holds tension and smile there. Continue this to the top of the head.

This restfulness of soul exercise has the purpose of laying down our daily gripping of personal will by using the release in the body, so that we may give all of ourselves to the exercises that come from meditative schooling.

It is informative to see our relationship to each of these exercises. Which are easy for us? Which are difficult? What are the differences between them? Before the meditative practice begins, the restfulness of soul exercise is chosen because it helps to put our everyday activities to one side. We choose which of the exercises best serves to put the workaday self to one side, for that is their purpose.

Many people skip the rest exercise; they tend to find that after going through all the verses and mantras, they have come to a restfulness of soul. It is indeed beneficial for the soul to find rest in this way, and yet restfulness is the place from which we need to begin our inner work if we really wish to strengthen the soul and gain from the schooling gifts.

Sitting is a balanced body position between the polarities of standing and lying down. When we go to sleep at night, to let go of our wakeful day-consciousness, we lie down. We let go of all that we think we are to reunite with all that we truly are, a gesture of surrender. When we are standing, we activate our attention. We stand in ourselves, awake and assertive. Standing can be useful for those who easily fall asleep during meditative exercises, and can prevent dozing off; but sitting is the balanced position that we want to work toward. If we are unable to let go of ourselves, we can begin the rest exercise lying down. On the other hand, if we are unable to hold powerful attention, particularly if we feel ourselves moving toward sleep, we should stand for the rest exercise. Ideally and in time, the sitting position, with its reflected balance, will be taken. It can take several months before we experience putting ourselves to one side. We do not need to wait to accomplish this before we move on to the verse. However, the true benefits are amplified once we are capable of beginning our meditation practice from this place in our soul.

The Verse as the Direction

The universal form of meditative practice utilizes a verse that directs the student's soul toward the higher self and the divine spiritual world. In this foundational practice we are not attempting to inquire into a particular realm of spiritual activity. We are directing ourselves toward the highest in us. Turning the soul away from the sense world toward the spiritual world is the next step.

First the soul is loosened from its everyday activity. Then the soul turns toward the divine. The verse must contain pictures of this image that support this turning toward the divine. There are many other daily verses that remind us of the divine in the world but are not used as the direction. The meditative verse in this form is the direction toward what lies beyond the sense world. The direction we head in is very important at the early stages of our development because we have to pass through what is known as the elemental or astral world. This elemental world is full of images, both of the spiritual world and of human thought content. We pass through this realm of consciousness when dreaming during sleep. As in the dream world, what lives in us affects what is drawn to us. What lives in us changes what presents itself to us in this realm of consciousness. It will take much effort before the soul is purified to the extent that it will not alter the images arising from the elemental world.

The true spiritual world has two realms; they are known in the Eastern schooling as Lower Devachan and Upper Devachan. These two realms lie beyond the elemental plane and are not interfered with by earthly perceptions as is the elemental plane. Yet this elemental plane has to be passed through to reach the true spiritual world; the verse can be the bridge that allows an unhindered crossing. The elemental world can create all kinds of diversions for the student. The thoughts of human beings continue to exist here. The emotions of human beings are born here, and the consciousness of the animal kingdom resides here. It is the atmosphere surrounding the earth. To navigate this atmosphere requires the capacity to read not only the image, but what lives behind the image; to recognize what creates the image. The theosophist Madame Blavatsky stated that there were many Buddhas walking the astral plane, built out of the thoughts of human beings. To read the images correctly requires soul capacities that are yet to be developed in the student. These capacities can take lifetimes to develop, or can open up relatively quickly. As another famous Theosophist, Sabba Row, indicated, it could take seven months, seven years or seven lifetimes; but if we work diligently it will happen. We will awaken to the true spiritual world and the beings behind the images of the elemental plane.

Becoming fascinated with the elemental plane of consciousness will waylay and even hinder inner development. This is the arena of psychics, who pick up the thoughts, wishes, and desires of human beings in their attachments to the sense world. Such activity makes the supposed spiritual world just like the physical world, and in doing so, threatens to bring into being an even greater materialism; as so often seen, spiritualists can become the greatest materialists. The genuine student avoids fascinating experiences, placing seeking the truth as the higher striving. The appropriate verse is given out of the eternal, a gift for the soul in the direction of divine truth. Here we have two verses that Steiner presented frequently to groups of students.

(1)

More radiant than the sun,
Purer than the snow,
Finer than the ether
Is the Self
The Spirit in my heart of hearts.
I am this Self.
This Self am I.

(2)

In purest outpoured light
Shimmers the Godhead of the World.
In purest love toward all that is
Outpours the godhood of my soul.
I rest within the Godhead of the World;
There shall I find myself
Within the Godhead of the World.[14]

There are several keys in working with the verse. Outside the meditation we cultivate a relationship to the verse. We deeply contemplate each line, opening up more and more depth. The verse becomes like a dear friend. Over the years, it reveals more to us; the friendship deepens. Just as our soul lifts on meeting a dear friend, so it lifts even at the thought of uniting with the verse. During the meditative practice we let the words of the verse pass through our souls; our thinking is with the words, the thoughts of the verse. Our feelings are moved to an experience like an inner speech, which changes the pattern of the air with each sound and each line. Immersed in the practice, our will unites with the verse. The more we give ourselves to the verse, the more its forces work on us. We must give it all of our thinking, all of our feeling, all of our willing, along with our awareness, enthusiasm, and warmth.

It is possible that one day we will not only think this verse and feel this verse, but we will also know it for ourselves to be the truth, as we have united with it. The verse itself can guide us to this experience. In its present use, in this form of meditative practice, its purpose is to turn the soul in the direction of the divine.

The Main Exercise: Cultivating Independent Soul Activity

Now that the soul is turned away from the sense world and toward the spiritual world, we can begin to strengthen the soul capacities independently of our bodily nature. It is important that we do not use the meditative exercises as personality maneuvers, as a way to increase our sense of the "me" self. The reverence for the divine that has been cultivated in the verse and the turning of the soul to the divine safeguard us to some degree from gaining personal ground from meditation, but we must always be on the lookout for this inclination. Strong weeds grow in fertile soil.

In his book *Knowledge of the Higher Worlds*, Steiner defines three stages of soul development: preparation and purification, enlightenment, and initiation. As we work upon each one, we do not simply move on to the next, but rather add, the next level. Preparation and purification continue throughout all other stages. While we are citizens of the earth we participate in the realm where adverse forces have permission to work. Materialism and egotism are present at every turn. It is better that we assume their presence rather than think we are free from such forces. In the Hermetic schooling it is said that we must watch the watcher, judge the judge, examine the examiner.

There are several main exercises presented by Steiner in the early esoteric classes. In studying them, we can assess the exercises we are working with and attempt to recognize how and where they work. The mantras given in the esoteric schooling are both verse and main exercise in one. The mantra includes, among other gifts, the image or thought for the sentient soul; the sequencing of thoughts and images for the intellectual soul; and an extra stimulus to the consciousness soul, which is the rhythm. This means that the translation into another language, which loses this rhythm, weakens this component of the gift of the mantra. However, the mantra works as powerfully in any language if the students are able to provide the necessary soul activity themselves. This is a secret to all esoteric work; nothing lies concealed if the candidate is ready. In fact the mantra can call up greater experience for the students who must provide aspects out of themselves. It is also a law that nothing can be revealed if the requisite soul faculties are not active; in this case the mantra, as with all other meditative exercises, serves to cultivate those requisite soul faculties. The advanced mantras direct inquiry into specific areas of spiritual wisdom, whereas these early exercises cultivate the universal soul capacities through an archetypal path.

THE ROSE CROSS MEDITATION

I

Death and resurrection comprise the journey of the evolving soul. We die to the outer self, and yet those forces utilized by the outer self do not die. Nothing truly dies, but only changes form. Resurrection is death followed by a higher level of consciousness. What has died is transformed to the higher step of soul development. This process is a picture of evolution. The evolving soul must die to itself as it is and be reborn at a higher level of wakefulness. The Rose Cross meditation, as given by Steiner in his book *Outline of Esoteric Science*, is both an imagination and an inspiration exercise.[15] Inspiration is cultivated during the preparation for the exercise, a stage that is often overlooked. The student prepares outside the meditation time.

In preparation, we compare ourselves with the world of plants. We see how more advanced the human being is: we can think, feel, and act independently. Compared with the plant world, we are so much more developed; and yet a plant, given the right conditions, will always reach its full flowering, its potential for this life. The purity of the plant does not affect its "God willed" intention to flower. It will be all that it is designed to be. This may not be the case for a human being. Because we have free will, we may choose to live out a personal desire, live in our passions. In comparison to the purity of the plant sap, these passions are carried by the blood in the human being. Even though human beings are always given the right conditions required to evolve, it may be that we do not evolve. We may not necessarily reach our flowering, our higher intention for this incarnation.

In this preparation, a feeling arises and is cultivated in the soul of the student; the plant contemplation imbues the student with a certain feeling. This feeling is like a solemn assent, an agreement that we will take this journey of evolving. It is this feeling that Steiner said is important to hold, as well as the image of the Rose Cross itself. It takes strong effort for us to hold the soul in this deepened feeling toward evolving. This feeling for the truth develops the capacity for inspiration. To hold this feeling in difficult life circumstances, to recognize that behind all outer appearance is the call for soul evolution, is much harder when the soul is bound to the preferences of liking and disliking, of wanting and not wanting.

The Rose Cross image is imbued with meaning. The black wooden cross with seven red roses is given meaning through us in this preparation. The blood is the bearer of our free will and our passions; and because of these passions, we may not take the journey of evolving. The roses represent the purified blood. We must enter willingly into this purification process. We must willingly wish to transform, to purify. The seven red roses, formed in a ring around the cross, represent the transformed blood. The black wooden cross represents all that needs to be transformed. This image is not one that we find in nature. It is important that the soul cultivate this image out of the depths of itself. It will not serve us to Google the Rose Cross and to use an image from memory.

During the meditation, after inwardly reciting the verse, which is the direction through the elemental realm, the student builds an image of the Rose Cross. We do not add our opinions about what within us needs to be transformed and put aside. We do not say, "I want to transform this or that," for we are not that wise. Rather, this image represents without words or ideas from the sense world an image in soul language. Upon the cross we lay seven red roses in a ring around the point where the two arms of the cross meet. We hold this image of the Rose Cross and the feeling that the preparation has awakened—the feeling that the soul affirms this journey. This image is held powerfully with all our soul's activity. The meditation is not done by the clock, but instead is held for as long as the soul can stay directed, fully engaged in the exercise.

2

Seven bright rose stars
On a black wooden cross;
Seven powerful soul forces
in the welter of life: strength, peace, striving for wisdom,
the power of love, detachment, attention, trust.
With these signs I inscribe my soul.[16]

This meditation focuses more strongly on inspiration. With this exercise we work with the soul powers as words of power. Various esoteric schools work with these soul forces, sometimes named slightly differently; it is not the name but the activity that counts. Just as we did with the sun and moon exercise, we drink in and become the activity of strength, peace, striving for wisdom, and so on. Some of these forces will resonate more clearly than others. Through soul activity, we can recognize the quality of inspiration of this exercise. Here we are inscribing the soul with the activity. There are images in this exercise, but it is dominated by activity that is without image. Therefore, we should not create an image for strength or peace, for example; rather, we should become the force of strength, become the activity of peace. These words of power prepare the soul for inspiration.

3

Imagine a black wooden cross surrounded by seven red roses. One by one, each rose becomes an illuminated white light, leaves the cross, and is placed on the body. With each placement the student inwardly lives into each invocation.

The first rose lights up the left side of the head:
"May your warmth warm through me."

The second rose lights up the right side of the head:
"May your light shine through me."

The third rose lights up the left hand:
"May your awakeness stream through me."

The fourth rose lights up the right hand:
"May your peace pour through me."

The fifth rose lights up the left foot:
"May your ray move powerfully through me."

The sixth rose lights up the right foot:
"May your raising up penetrate me."

The seventh rose lights up above the head:
"I am in your sphere." [17]

This meditation works more strongly with intuition preparation. The focus is on the activity of uniting ourselves with the image. The rose transforms, and we become one with it. Using our own body, the ground of the consciousness soul, this exercise supports the foundation for intuition.

Comparing these three Rose Cross exercises, we can experience the differences that we are being supported to develop. The first Rose Cross exercise is the most widely used; if we are capable of giving ourselves fully to this exercise for several minutes, we may then choose, through self-knowledge, another exercise, according to which capacity we need to develop. Once this has been achieved, which may take several months of active inner work, then we may be ready for the next form of the meditative practice: extinguishing what we have built up.

EXTINGUISHING THE IMAGE
Opening to Spiritual Imagination

Before we can extinguish anything, we must have created it. We must have brought it forth out of our own soul activity. Even though the Rose Cross exercise is given from the spiritual world, we have to create it inwardly out of our own soul forces that are freed from their body-bound activity. Therefore, we should not jump to extinguishing the image until we have strengthened the activity of creating it. If we extinguish an image that has not been called forth from our own soul forces, we may run into two difficulties. First, we will not be able to extinguish the image, and it will continue to come forth even if it takes on changing forms. Second, we will find our souls filling up with either earthly thought or elemental thought. We will find ourselves drawn into materialistic thoughts or egotistic illusions.

When we are able, we should not delay in taking the step of extinguishing the image. This step requires the ability to drop seeing the image but to continue the soul activity that produced the image. In earthly terms we could use this expression "looking without seeing," or "listening without hearing." The effort of looking continues, but we look at nothing. The effort of hearing continues, but we hear silence. All that we needed to do to create the image continues to be active. The force behind the image remains, but the image itself is extinguished. This can be likened to the experience of deep sleep consciousness, but while we remain fully conscious.

EXTINGUISHING TO EMPTY CONSCIOUSNESS
Opening to Spiritual Inspiration

The next step requires that we now extinguish the activity, the effort we have made out of ourselves. This is uncommon for the soul, because it is used to being occupied. To stay present in and of itself requires tremendous strength. Yet the empty soul is the soul that is available for something else to enter. It is not uncommon for the student to say, "I did not know whether I was asleep or awake in that moment of emptiness." It is not uncommon for the student to say, "The moment I thought I had it, I lost it." To begin with, empty consciousness is foreign. We are no longer full of ourselves, yet we are not strong enough in soul to maintain awareness in the emptiness. Finally, after many months or even years of practice, the student is capable of staying present in emptiness.

It is easy for the soul to lose consciousness at this point, for unless it has gained sufficient strength, it will enter a kind of sleep. This is quite normal at the start, and we do not need to fear what will occur at that point of sleep. It will feel like replenishment even if our consciousness does not follow us where we go. It is said that it can be harmful to fall asleep during meditation, but this is not the case in the extinguishing part of the meditation, or the rest exercises.

It is not useful—and it is even depleting—to fall asleep during the verse and main exercises, because in those we are trying to strengthen the soul actively, out of ourselves, by giving ourselves fully to the exercise. If we fall asleep, it is a sign that the adverse or diverting forces in us are gaining the upper hand, which runs counter to our purpose and commitment in doing the exercises. In this case, we must be vigilant not to sleep during the verse or main exercise.

From this place we can cleanly cross the threshold into the spiritual world, and this full surrender is the hardest of all. In empty consciousness, the consciousness soul is all that remains. It is deeply strengthening to be in this oasis of nothing; and to begin with it can be terrifying. The soul is not accustomed to this nothingness, this black-bedecked darkness.

Once the soul finds its footing, this nothingness becomes an oasis from the clamor of life, from the clamor of the "me" self. We feel more truly ourselves in this emptiness than in any other relationship in our life. Yet this, too, must be surrendered to take the next step, where the point becomes the periphery and yet stays in and aware of itself.

Surrendering

To cross into the spiritual world, the consciousness soul unites with the Spiritual Self. This requires another surrendering. It may have us quaking in our boots. No one comes to this point without initially fearing that nothing exists, that nothing will be on the other side— including ourselves. Darkness surrounds us and we need to enter willingly. Many students of meditation reach this point and go no further, not because they are held back by the spiritual world but because this final surrender appears to be death to the soul. The eighth-century Sufi saint, Rabia of Basra, said in "Die before You Die":

> Ironic, but one of the most intimate acts
> of our body is
> death.
>
> So beautiful appeared my death—knowing who then I
> would kiss,
> I died a thousand times before I died.
>
> "Die before you die," said the Prophet
> Muhammad.
>
> Have wings that feared ever
> touched the Sun?
>
> I was born when all I once
> feared—I could
> love. [18]

It is a grace to be allowed entry into this realm of the spiritual world because help comes from the spirit itself. No human being can insist upon this entry, but we can prepare our souls; we can ensure that we have gathered enough of our own soul light to illuminate the way. We can prepare the way so that we are available if it is in our destiny to receive it.

Through this crossing we may experience true spiritual intuition, the first awakening into the higher spiritual world; unity with continual consciousness. Then we know who we truly are. We know that there is no death. We know that only the spirit is. In Rosicrucian teachings it is expressed thus: "I am nothing in myself, I am everything in thee, and I live in thine everything from nothing. Live Thou then in me, and so bring me unto the All in Thee."[19]

This first crossing is sometimes termed the birth of the higher "I," the higher self. The way has been found. Many have this experience and think that this is all there is, that illumination has been achieved. They may even want to tell the world about the "truth" and become a teacher of the path. In reality, this is just the first step. The path has just opened out. Then comes the great work of transformation, of transforming all the forces that live in us and placing them in service of the divine.

3

The Enlightenment of the Soul

Contemplation, meditation, and esoteric exercises strengthen the soul. The soul requires strengthening so that it is able to live independently of the outer body. The soul is the aspect of the human being that is in relationship to the spiritual world. The free soul is consciously in relationship to the spiritual world. To know for ourselves that the spiritual world exists and that we are citizens of that world is essential for the soul's ongoing evolution. As the saying goes, "If I was king, but did not know I was king, would I be king?" Would I be able to be true to my essential being and my task?

Just as the individual requires a body with functioning sense organs in order to participate in the physical world, so does the individual require a soul body with functioning faculties to participate in the soul-spiritual world. The organs of the body that allow perceptions of the sense-perceptible world are present at birth and grow unconsciously, whereas the soul's capacities that allow perception of the soul-spiritual world must be actively cultivated. Individual human beings must do for themselves what takes place unconsciously in the plant. Out of our own efforts, we must come to our blossoming.

The greatest strengthening of our soul and the greatest schooling for developing spiritual capacities come not only from inner exercises but indeed from life itself—from the life that lives inside us and outside us, and is our individual schooling. Life is the greatest gift for the evolving soul; without it we would not develop the many capacities required for our awakening, greatest of which is the capacity to love, the creative life-sustaining power that is the substance of the divine spiritual world.

Your individual life reflects all that your individual soul needs to develop and overcome. Your individual life will show you your errors and your deficiencies, and will guide you along the path of becoming a being of love. Your individual life always supports the development of the required capacities. It supports the capacities of wisdom and knowledge that in this incarnation you are working to acquire from various dimensions. These capacities are developed through three main activities in the schooling of life: overcoming of materialism, overcoming of egotism, and the ongoing relationship toward and development of the higher "I." The first is overcoming of materialism and our over-binding to the material world. Not only is the soul bound to the outer self, but it is also bound to the outer world. This outer sense world is not recognized as maya, as the shell of the spiritual world. Because of materialistic thinking, the sense world seems for most souls to be a greater reality than the spiritual world it hides.

Just as the physical body becomes the "true self," so does the physical world become the "true world." This misconception, this illusion, has to be surmounted before the soul can be liberated. It is in this continual overcoming that the soul gains the capacities required to perceive the spiritual world. Maya is essential to the development of these soul capacities. The soul needs to meet the sensory world and rise above the illusion of it. Without the sense-born world the soul would not, through the overcoming of it, develop the capacities to recognize the truth. The soul would not be able to distinguish the essential from the nonessential without overcoming it. It would not be able to differentiate the transient from the eternal. Without the earthly journey, the powers of the inner divine would lie dormant. Through this journey of life we may come to recognize the spiritual.

The second activity that all developing individuals must work upon in our times through the sphere of life is the overcoming of egotism and selfishness. In true meditation we find in ourselves this egotistical being. The path of meditation does not lead us to be rocked in comfort and ease, but rather brings us to meet all that lives in us. We see many things that we would rather not admit. We like to overestimate ourselves, have power over others, and always be seen as right. We desire comfort and ease over transformation and truth. We are full of vanities and prejudices. We find many shortcomings in our soul when we meditate deeply.

Many people use meditation as a way of de-stressing so that they can continue their lives in the same way, almost like having a glass of wine to relax from the workday. They do not want meditation to tear them away from their comforts, their usual way of living (which may be the cause of the stress); rather, they want their meditative life to bring them more comfort so that they can continue their imbalanced way of being. They want their meditation practice to support life in their own way, with their sympathies and antipathies, with their desires and preferences, with their self-will remaining unchanged.

Some others use the path of spiritual development to beautify themselves, to gain the perfect yoga body, in order to appear as though they posses spiritual qualities. This is an egotistical use of meditative exercises. The student of meditation who uses exercises to maintain the everyday self will also use life in the same way, for self-gain rather than for meaningful transformation. "All knowledge pursued merely for the enrichment of personal learning and the accumulation of personal treasure leads you away from the path; but all knowledge pursued for growth to ripeness within the process of human ennoblement and cosmic development brings you a step forward."[20]

This self-seeking must be overcome because in the spiritual world these egotistical forces cause deception. We must encounter ourselves, face all that lives in us. Only honest self-appraisal is of value, not in order to diminish ourselves, but in order to distinguish the true from the false, the beautiful from the ugly, the good from the immoral. If we are unable to become aware of these egotistical things within us, it will be impossible to recognize them outside us. Without this honest self-appraisal and ability to differentiate, we are potentially giving rise to deceptions that in the physical world can be easily corrected, but when passing into the soul-spiritual world will cause great uncertainty, present diversions, and hinder true progress.

The third activity is our ongoing development of the higher "I." We may not be conscious of this higher "I," this true, divine self, yet it is working continuously in our life—both in our inner life and in our external life. In developing our relationship to it, we learn to see our unfolding life experiences differently. We learn to listen more inwardly. We can no longer blame the other—another person, outer circumstances, that otherness we hold responsible for our experiences. Steiner gives us a picture: Imagine walking along and a slate falls off a roof and hits you on the head. We have to imagine that we ourselves pushed the slate off the roof. We must consider that our higher being calls up for us all of our life experiences.

This other self weaves our destiny, and at the same time we are confronted with choices within this destiny that we need to act upon, to which we need to respond. This is occurring continuously in life. It is up to us to develop our faculties to distinguish the higher choice so that we may make the decision to take action for the evolutionary path. Yet we are still free even when we see the evolutionary path; we are free to choose whether or not to take it. The higher "I" inwardly always leaves us free.

These three development steps that are cultivated in life are not independent of one another and are developed simultaneously; but each has its own quality and brings forth its own soul capacity. There are various exercises that support the awareness of these three activities. This awareness can be gained in life itself; but owing to the powerful obstacles of materialism and egotism in our outer and inner life, we often cannot develop it without first training the soul. "The difficulty in this case is due to the fact that these obstacles, though affecting the course of the soul's inner experience, are not apprehended as such by ordinary consciousness."[21]

To gain insight into the inner experience of these three soul activities and thus to help us recognize them in the throes of life, we can study and practice the esoteric exercises that speak directly to soul experience. We practice them so that we can have an individual relationship to them. We need to see for ourselves how the exercises work upon our soul, so that we may choose the exercises that are the most useful for us. We study the exercises so that we may understand the development of the human soul. What has been given in esoteric schooling is training for the future development of humanity.

We can faithfully take on an exercise, and just do it; but more is gained today if we can see how an exercise is working upon us and what its effects are—what it is cultivating within. By understanding the effects of the exercises, we understand the path itself. It is useful to investigate the exercise for ourselves, as we have passed beyond the point where we can look toward a guru or leader, and in so doing become a follower. Human evolution has passed beyond that point, and we are at a new stage of development. We can, however, be supported by a teacher in the same way that a student of art may be supported by an art teacher. Art teachers can give certain instructions and indicate their experience of working with a particular modality. They may speak of helps and hindrances in the work. They may facilitate practical lessons. But the art teacher also remains aware that it is essential for art students to develop their own expression and unique style.

The so-called student is walking an individual path potentially to very different ground than the so-called teacher. This fundamental truth underlies Western esoteric schooling and is stated in *Knowledge of the Higher Worlds:* "Each human being can alone awaken this higher being within the self." The more we penetrate the exercises, the more we learn about the evolution of human beings. The more we learn about the evolutionary path, the more we understand what the exercises are helping to cultivate. The more we recognize the inner work, the more we realize how the outer world supports us, guides us, and awakens us. The more we come to know the outer world, the more we perceive the spiritual world. It is a continuing journey with no fixed goal.

We are evolving beings. We are in the process of becoming. We can discover wisdom that already exists, but for this to become our living wisdom and not just intellectual knowledge, we must evolve. "Learning is not the basis for training someone who is becoming a disciple, in the higher sense of genuine esotericism; rather, all learning of esoteric science occurs within the etheric body. Consequently, if you have managed to transform any firmly rooted characteristic, you have done more for a true esoteric training then you would by acquiring any amount of external knowledge."[22]

Higher "I" perception and development has several supporting exercises, one of which is creating time for inner tranquility. This calm, this serenity, assists the growth of the inner human being. When a pebble is thrown into turbulent waters, we do not perceive its effects, but when it is thrown into still, calm waters, we do perceive its effects. Initially, the higher "I" is inwardly perceived out of this tranquility. "Esoteric pupils should free themselves from all external influences surrounding them; not in order to flee the world, but rather in order to make their own true higher 'I,' the spiritual self, the true human being within, independent."[23]

It is difficult in the pace of life in our Western society to naturally find inner tranquility. This may appear as a great hindrance to the path of inner development. Yet all hindrances are really supports because the soul develops mighty strengths through overcoming them. Without the strength gained from overcoming so-called hindrances, the soul would not develop enough strength to be able to take its next step on the path.

A hindrance is in itself an image of what needs to be strengthened. Study your hindrances, for they reveal to you where your individual work lies. Some hindrances are archetypal to the path, and we all will need to overcome them, while others are individual to you. The hindrance of finding inner calm and tranquility is a universal one. "No outward forces can supply space to the inner human being. It can only be supplied by the inner calm that we ourselves give to our Soul."[24]

From this place of inner tranquility, we can view our outer life as well as our responses to our circumstances as though we are looking at another's life. We can take stock of our life without the common subjectivity. We can begin to perceive this higher self working in our life's unfolding. We can begin to say "I" not only to our self-consciousness but also to our biography. We can stand back, observing the mysterious threads that weave the life that we are experiencing. It is in this state of inner calm that we perceive the higher "I" at work in our outer life.

As the Sufi poet Hafiz tells us in his poem "For a While":

> We have come to the right place.
> We all sit in God's classroom.
>
> Now,
> The only thing left for us to do, my dear,
> Is to stop
> Throwing spitballs for a while.[25]

To perceive the quality of the higher "I" at work in our inner life, we can employ another exercise. Every day we make decisions that lead us through our lives. If our intention is to respond to life in a way that is evolutionary, then we need to seek in ourselves that evolving being and its qualities. We must cultivate a quality of recognition, discerning the true path forward, not by words but by experiencing the rightness of a decision or choice. The Y exercise is particularly useful for this.

Imagine a circle divided into three equal parts. Then take away the outer circle, and you are left with a Y shape. On the upper arm extending to the left, the words "command me" are written. On the upper arm extending to the right, the words "forbid me" are written. On the center line nothing is written. Bring to mind a decision, a choice that needs to be made. Work from the center of the Y to the periphery: on the "command me" line think through all the reasons to say "yes" to this decision. It is important to try to make these thoughts run in a logical sequence. Place effort into this logical sequencing and do not just allow several thoughts to jump in. Rather, spend time organizing these thoughts. Then do the same thing on the "forbid me" line. Think through all the reasons you can find for not making this choice, again by organizing your thoughts and bringing out into consciousness your inner sympathies and antipathies.

Once you have exhausted what you are aware of thinking about this choice that needs to be made, hold the symbol in your mind's eye and focus your attention on the center arm of the Y. You will experience a quality that arises from this center line. The higher "I" neither commands nor forbids us in life, but we experience an inner knowing, a rightness, a recognition. This quality of recognition becomes perceptible to the soul, sometimes like a whisper and sometimes like an iron rod of knowing. We will perceive the higher way for us to take in this presenting circumstance. This quality develops through regularly engaging the exercise until we feel in the speed of life that we can discern the higher path consistently in daily choices. Whether we choose this higher way depends on us. Even when we can recognize the evolving way, even when we have a clear sense of the rightness of a choice, we do not necessarily choose it; but it is here that we hear the many inner voices at work, and we have our freedom to listen to any of them. This exercise, using the events in our outer life, helps us to distinguish the higher "I" working in our inner life.

Overcoming egotism is a collective challenge in self-development. The nature of this path requires self-reliance, self-evaluation, and self-control, which enhance the individualized ego. Self-development requires the fullness of the individuality. The ego can be like a double-edged sword: "From one point of view, it causes people to grow inwardly hard, to draw into the service of the ego all that may be available to them in the form either of outer things or inner capacities.... The ego also makes us independent, gives us our inner freedom, which in the truest sense of the word elevates and exalts us. Our worth and dignity are founded in this ego. It is our potential for the divine."[26]

The qualities of self-reliance and self-control required to attain inner knowledge can become great hindrances to our inner work. The small book *Light on the Path* helps us to understand the useful form of such qualities. We are instructed, for example, to kill out ambition, yet to live life as though we were ambitious. We must employ the same forces as the ambitious person, but not on behalf of ourselves. Kill out the desire for life, and yet respect life as those do who desire it. In a world intent on devouring through desire, we must continue to live with respect for life.

One of the ways of overcoming egotism is to choose which voice you listen to and whom you are working for: to work for the self sharpens one edge of the ego; to work on behalf of the other sharpens the other edge. The ego is tricky in this respect; people often imagine themselves working with selflessness when even that is gratifying a personal desire. The ego finds it difficult to give up its self-gain. Hafiz tells us, in "Manic Screaming":

> We should make all spiritual talk
> Simple today:
>
> God is trying to sell you something,
> But you don't want to buy.
>
> That is what your suffering is:
> Your fantastic haggling,
> Your manic screaming over the price! [27]

In developing the capacities of the soul, we must humbly work with the words that Steiner often quoted: "When the rose adorns itself, it also adorns the garden." At the same time we must become vigilant to our tricky ego: "In everyday life people allow their actions to be decided by what satisfies them personally, by what bears fruit for themselves. In so doing, they force upon the world's events the direction of their personality. They do not bring to realization the truth that is traced out in the laws of the spiritual world; rather do they realize the demands of their self-will."[29] Many exercises are given to help in the overcoming of our egotism, yet at the same time strengthen our egohood. The six subsidiary exercises are invaluable in this respect. They develop strength and solidity in our egohood, while avoiding feeding our egotism.

In working upon the existing egotism that arises in our everyday life encounters, the Rose Cross symbol is extremely valuable. It can be used not only as a main meditative exercise, as described in chapter 2, but also in life events. If we become entangled in our daily life and feel ourselves defending our personal self, our own thoughts and ideas, unable to be objective and clear, we can call upon the Rose Cross symbol. In our daily life, with eyes open, we inwardly imagine the Rose Cross symbol and at the same time bring forth the cultivated feeling of wanting to walk the path of dying and becoming. We make use of the feeling that also is cultivated in the main exercise of the Rose Cross. The Rose Cross is a soul image that speaks of the path we must walk; it is full of riches for the soul's learning.

This dying and becoming, in which the ego must willingly participate, are central to this symbol. When we call upon this symbol, which is also a protective symbol, we disentangle ourselves from the influences that come to us from the outer world. All so-called protective symbols call upon our own powers of disentanglement, which in turn close the door to harmful influences: "We pour all influences from the outer world into this sheath ego; they tear and pull us back and forth. All influences that go from one person to another in the way just indicated hit the sheath ego. We must try to strengthen the true, real 'I' that far surpasses the other one. Then we are immune to outer influences."[30]

If we find that we have become caught in our emotions, then we have to work to free ourselves again. We should not imagine that as we strengthen ourselves we weaken our tendency toward strong emotions, to prejudices and the forces of our personal will. In fact, the opposite is true. "We have to strengthen our sense of self if we wish to rise into the spiritual world. But in the process of strengthening our sense of self, we also strengthen all the tendencies, habits, weaknesses, and prejudices that are held back and limited in the external world through our education, through custom, and through the outward culture."[29] Emotions that we engage with are soul powers that have become personalized. The activity that streams through our souls is in constant flux, like the planets in their continual movement through their various positions and conjunctions; it is not personal emotion, but rather experience that is acquired by allowing the activity that streams in us to be witnessed, experienced, and learned from.

An exercise that helps free our emotions is this one: In our private space, we recall inwardly the events that have become personal to us. First, we imagine as vividly as possible all the outer circumstances—the time of year, the surrounding place, the clothes we were wearing, what others were wearing, the atmosphere, and so on. We allow ourselves to really feel the emotion, and then we step back as an observer of our own soul activity. We do not stop feeling, but we now also watch the feeling. We find our inner equanimity, not by dulling what we feel, but rather by not being bound in a personal way to what we are experiencing. The power, the energy, that we were personalizing is now freed and is transformed through our new attention. It can become a revealing experience.

Indeed, it can become the ground for spiritual feeling, or inspiration. Personal feeling is limiting because we feel what we already have experienced; whereas spiritual inspiration allows the new to be experienced. This exercise releases us from personal entanglement with the event, an entanglement that prevents us from being in a state of learning.

As Goethe said, "As long as thou art without this 'dying and becoming', thou art but an uneasy guest on the dark Earth."[31] What must die is this sheath "I"; what must become is the true "I."

———

Every event happens in order to show us something; the spiritual world is alive in each moment, living in each event. Memory that we use in order to find the new and the living can serve the "true I" in us. Memory for the personalized past serves the "sheath I" that wants to continuously reconstruct itself, its life, its way. Only if we use memory to find what is new in each moment does the past become helpful in our evolution. This takes place through the ability to perceive the new experience where living spiritual life is at work. By using memory to respond from the past, where most personal emotions arise; by judging the present situation from the past, where most personal thinking arises; by acting according to the past, where most personal actions arise, we limit ourselves to what is known, and we also keep our small ego intact. Memory can be the backdrop that allows us to see the living expression in the present situation. The spiritual is always living, ever new. To find the spirit, we must seek the living expression, which is not a memory. Every moment contains this living expression, yet some moments are greater teachings.

The caduceus symbol helps us in inwardly overcoming materialism and materialistic thinking. This protective symbol can be used to stop materialistic thoughts from bombarding us, not only during meditative practice, but also in daily life when we are caught in materialistic thinking and perceiving. Two snakes, one black and one shimmering white, curl equally around a golden staff. The black snake represents the devouring force of material life that confronts us every day. The white snake represents our renewed being, which is revitalized in our sleep and which is our unconscious reuniting with the spiritual world. We create this picture in our mind's eye, but we focus our attention on the golden staff. This golden staff represents the true "I," the higher "I." The balancing activity of this

"I" harmonizes the polarities. Through this symbol the soul experiences a quality of the higher "I."

Symbols are extremely potent for the soul because they bypass our intellectual brain thinking and speak directly to the soul's unfolding. Symbols are not arbitrarily made up, but represent the soul's evolution in picture, in sign, in soul language. The initiates gave these symbols as teachings in esoteric schooling. The soul embraces the symbol and learns through these signs. Every symbol has many secrets, which, as the soul develops its capacities over time, reveal more to the student. It is the same in everyday life, when a soul with greater capacities will inwardly experience much from a beautiful evening sunset, while another soul is hardly touched. We can see this development of capacities in ourselves. We may read an important esoteric work, and come back to it several years later to find that the same book reveals deeper mysteries. The words on the page have not changed, but we have changed. The greater the esoteric work, the more these mysteries require our transformation to comprehend them.

Other exercises that help in the overcoming of materialism are the various nature kingdom contemplation exercises. There are many such exercises, but what they all have in common is that they help us experience what is behind the physical appearance of things. They help us recognize the different consciousness of each kingdom and how these kingdoms relate in spiritual activity to varying states of consciousness within the human being.

The living plant and the dying plant exercise begins with choosing two trees or plants—one that is living, growing, and flourishing, and the other that is dying and decaying. The soul learns through comparison. It requires the polarities so that it may understand the differences. When we do any nature exercise, we are also attempting to see the inner effects of the outer appearance. In the living and dying plant exercise we observe how these two processes of life and death affect us in different ways. While looking at the living tree, we keep watch on our inner life, our inner experience. Then, for a few minutes, we shift our gaze to the dying tree, keeping part of our awareness on what we are experiencing. It is usually in the chest area that the experience is felt most clearly.

As citizens of the sense world, we open up our senses and direct them to what we wish to observe. I am here. The plant is over there. This duality of self and other is a law in the sense world. As I hold my awareness on the plants and also toward my inner experience, I can perceive how the inner activity of the living plant is very different from the inner activity that is created by the dying plant. As I go back and forth between these two plants, one growing and flourishing, and the other dying and decaying, I recognize inwardly that different activities are produced. As a being of soul, I am experiencing the plants.

The living plant and the dying plant have activities that we then put into words in an attempt to describe them. Some may use the word *expansion* for the living plant and *contraction* for the dying plant. We can use various other expressions—opening and closing, lightness and heaviness—in trying to describe the inner activity of this outer process. Some may use the words *sadness* and *joy*. While the plant, however, is not sad or joyful, for us the activity we are experiencing is similar to what we feel in sadness and joy. But we try to avoid using expressions of human emotion so that we develop objectivity and not sympathy and antipathy. The plant is over there, but the activity is within us. We become aware that we are participating not only in the sense world, but also in the world of soul experience, where the laws of division are different. We become aware that we are participating simultaneously in this sense world and the soul world.

We are also citizens of the spiritual world. Although the sense world is the loudest, strongest experience while we are in our waking day-consciousness, if we direct our awareness to our soul's experience, we can experience beyond the sense world. To become aware of the spiritual activity, which is different from soul activity, we once again direct our senses to the sense world, to the living and dying plant, but now we keep our awareness on our consciousness.

Consciousness is usually experienced around the head area. Now as we move between the living plant and the dying plant, what is perceived is quite different from the perception of our soul activity. We no longer experience expansion and contraction like a streaming activity of feeling. Now when we observe what takes place in our consciousness around the head area, we recognize that one of these plants cultivated a greater awareness and wakefulness than the other. In the soul we may have a preference for the living plant, for the expansion, for the uplifting, but in our conscious life, where we find spiritual activity, the experience is different. The activity that the dying plant brings is greater wakefulness and clarity, when compared with the living, growing plant.

Herein lies one of the great mysteries of being human. The effects on the soul life are different from the effects on the life of spiritual consciousness. The mysteries of human suffering lie in this wisdom. Like all meditative exercises, this one reveals many layers. As we work with it, we can learn much about the human being, as well as the other beings we relate to. At the same time, we are being schooled in objectivity. We are being schooled in soul language.

Imagine living in a world where inner activity is stronger than outer perception. Imagine living in a world where inner experience is the strongest experience. We would no longer believe that the outer world is the most important world, and certainly not the only world. As a being of soul living in the soul world, these inner activities develop new sense organs. We no longer read with external sense perceptions what presents itself to us. The living, streaming, weaving, feeling, is soul activity. When we enter into the soul world, leaving behind the world of senses, we find it very difficult to orient ourselves unless we have developed a relationship to this soul world, developed our soul language and inner repertoire.

When we perceive the aura of a being, it is not that we see with our sense perceptions the color of that aura, but that we inwardly have the same experience that we would have if we were to see that color outwardly. How many of us have trained ourselves to recognize the soul activity of red, blue, or yellow? Life presents this schooling. Everything is laid out before us. All that we need to prepare ourselves is there in external life, but if we bind ourselves to the sense perception alone, we miss the inner teaching of things. We miss the training that is in front of us because we lose sight of our soul life and our spiritual life, while we believe more and more in the appearance of things in the physical life. If we prepare ourselves correctly before we enter into the soul world, we enter with our spiritual consciousness awake, aware. Then the soul world comes into view, and we are not lost in it, but instead awake and observing the inner streaming. We observe the soul's activity without sympathy and antipathy, but in a state of learning. We enter the temple of wisdom.

This simple plant or tree exercise prepares us, teaches us, and develops our capacities. It develops our inner language and library, which is essential in relating to the soul world. The student begins to utilize the sense world in a new way. The student starts to seek the soul activity that is behind everything manifest in the external world. If we are capable of distinguishing ourselves as beings of body, soul, and spirit, we can begin to experience not only the activity of the other being, but also the other being's consciousness. We can begin to experience the spiritual consciousness behind things. Then we begin to experience eternal truth. "It is well never to lose sight of the fact that, fundamentally, there is nothing in the universe but consciousness—consciousnesses. Everything outside the consciousness of beings—of whatever order—belongs to the realm of maya, the 'Great Illusion.'"[32]

The human being's consciousness manifests its awareness in its relationship to the earthly world. Although we may become aware of beings in other worlds, in other realms, our first awareness of our individual "I am" awakens in our earthly existence. The animal's consciousness is not manifest as a spiritual being in earthly existence, but the animal's consciousness as a spiritual consciousness exists in the elemental/astral world. The plant's consciousness as a spiritual consciousness exists in the Lower Devachan realm, and the mineral consciousness exists in the Upper Devachan realm. If we are able to unite our consciousness with the consciousness of the animal kingdom, the plant kingdom, or the mineral kingdom, we will experience the realm in which each consciousness resides.

Through meditative practice we experience these various realms of consciousness. Building an image in meditative exercises mirrors in us the elemental/astral world. Extinguishing the image, the verse, or the mantra, and being left with the pure activity of the soul alone, links us with the Lower Devachan world. This is the original home of the soul. Extinguishing all activity of soul, and thus being left with empty consciousness, links us with the Upper Devachan world. This is the original home of the spirit. These exercises utilize the outer world of things and help us recognize the different inner states of consciousness during meditation. They help us glimpse these realms of consciousness, and prepare us. At the same time, our meditative life develops in us a capacity to experience more deeply the consciousness of these other beings. The outer world changes for us as we recognize that we are surrounded by spiritual beings.

When we look out upon this manifested world, we see these various kingdoms: the human kingdom, the animal kingdom, the plant kingdom, and the mineral kingdom. We can become aware of these beings as forms of consciousness. In the physical world these four kingdoms all have a physical body. As we develop and awaken in ourselves, we recognize that there are also beings that do not manifest in a physical body in this physical world.

There are forms of consciousness that reside in the different realms of the soul-spiritual world. Not all beings manifest an outer body. Some beings can manifest their presence of thoughts, feelings, and actions in the elemental world even though their home is outside that world. The elemental world is closest to us. It is closest to our experience of our earthly consciousness because it expresses itself in pictures and images that are familiar to us, but still its laws are different from physical laws. In the physical world, the world of duality and division, I am separate from you. In the elemental world we merge with and unite with the other. We think, feel, and act like the being with whom we have merged. The only way we can learn in the elemental world is if our consciousness, our individualized "I" being, can stay present to the altered experience.

Humanity has begun to break through this threshold, the boundary between the physical and elemental world. If those who cross over are unprepared, we will see more mental disorders in our community. As fascination with the occult, psychic powers, and the supernatural continue to grow, all sorts of false paths of "inner development" will become more and more popular. Consciousness-altering substances that exploit a form of gate-crashing to enter the other dimensions will increase. Using these substances to enter different states of consciousness will be seen as an acceptable and inevitable path for our young people.

As we try to gain a foothold in the elemental world, which is coming into our consciousness as humanity crosses the threshold, whether we like it or not, or are ready or not, some of these footholds may not be progressive and strengthening, but backward pulling and weakening. Teaching meditation techniques to children may become acceptable, but it will lead ultimately to a weakened relationship to the spiritual world, and thereby leave them open to all sorts of potentially harmful influences by stepping backward, not forward, in their incarnating process. All those who truly know the path of inner development know that a healthy relationship to the spiritual world is acquired by completing all the necessary developmental stages of childhood first.

These various occurrences that we already see are signs that humanity is crossing this threshold unprepared. Rudolf Steiner describes this unprepared entry into the elemental world, likening it to putting your head into an ant's nest. Anyone who has experienced entering unprepared would not wish to lead others toward it in any unprepared way.

Preparing ourselves to enter healthily takes commitment and continual effort. Then we can enter consciously this "Hall of Learning," where wisdom is waiting to reveal itself. We need to be developing higher faculties of consciousness, whereby we may think in a direction and the thoughts or images come back to us, teaching us. We can ask questions in our soul and receive answers that are beyond our individual capacity. Although we personally do not know these things, they become known through us. We are receiving spiritual imaginations and inspirations.

This path is hard and narrow. Although many souls wish to reap the benefits of the path, they feel unable or unwilling to do the necessary work. Even though all obstacles that we face on the path are those that we ourselves have placed there, we still resist this great work. Many recognize that the time has come to take this step of responsibility. Humanity requires it of us, even though we do not feel ready or capable of taking this challenging journey. The fact is that it is happening. We are crossing this threshold, and that must become for us a call to quicken our evolution. We never feel ready for our next step, yet in the doing we become ready.

In "A Divine Invitation," Hafiz says:

> You have been invited to meet
> The Friend.
>
> No one can resist a Divine Invitation.
>
> That narrows down all our choices
> To just two:
>
> We can come to God
> Dressed for Dancing.
>
> Or,
>
> Or be carried on a stretcher
> To God's ward.[33]

Strengthening our individualized consciousness before working in the elemental world is essential. Everything that lives in us affects how the elemental world expresses itself through us. It is impossible to read the pictures of the elemental world without inner development.

Inner development allows us to recognize the being who creates the picture. A lustful being can create beautiful, enticing images. In the physical world, the morality of people is not obvious from their external appearance, yet our inner development can pick up the deceptiveness of a "nice looking" person. Plastic surgery for appearance alone may not resound inwardly as beautiful, because it is often based on materialistic thinking.

Whatever external facade we may give ourselves, our soul being shines through to those who have developed their inner faculties. The truth is revealed behind the external expression. This ability is required to a far greater degree in the elemental world. Even though the elemental world is the closest to our physical world, it is the least clear spiritually. Steiner tells us that this is not the true spiritual world, but rather carries the imprints and thoughts of spiritual beings.

It is important to know that not all spiritual beings are divine beings. Some are working toward diverting humanity from the path of evolution: increasing materialism, reinforcing egotism, magnifying our false self, deepening our lower ego. It is useful to recognize that these diverting beings can also support our premature access into the spiritual world. The path for humanity and for each one of us is to align freely with the beings of progression, the beings of the divine spiritual world. For that to be possible, we must find the progressive being, the divine being within ourselves.

We find many hindrances within us and outside us as we walk this path of development, but we can be assured that all hindrances are, in fact, a help. They help because in overcoming them our soul life is strengthened. We can gain the strength required only through overcoming these hindrances, and in truth this is a gift to us. As we begin to consciously walk this path, hindrances may arise that even prevent the practice of our meditative exercises. Every obstacle surmounted helps us take a step forward.

Not everything we find in the soul is to be overcome. As human beings, we also gather strength not only through transformation but also through bearing the human experience. Even in childhood these things that we must learn to bear come to us. One very difficult human experience is isolation, loneliness. It is the sign of consciousness soul development, and at some point all human beings will experience this—not because there is something wrong with us, and not because we have gone off track, but because we are human beings. Even in the most intimate relationship we can still experience that deep within we are alone. Often we blame ourselves for this experience; or we blame the other. We think that if only we were loved enough, we would not have this feeling. We think that if only we were lovable enough, we would not have this feeling. Teenagers can be deeply despairing when they first experience this isolation in its full power, which can reveal itself profoundly in those years.

We try to escape this isolation, to cover up the loneliness. We try to ignore it; at times it goes away, but it is a part of our human condition. As we age in life, we can become more at ease with this aloneness, but rarely do we find our right relationship to it. It is up to each one of us to find our own way of bearing these human experiences.

As Hafiz tells us in "Absolutely Clear":

Don't surrender your loneliness
So quickly,
Let it cut more deep.

Let it ferment and season you
As few human
Or even divine ingredients can.
Something missing in my heart tonight
Has made my eyes so soft,
My voice
So tender,
My need of God
Absolutely
Clear.[34]

The second experience that human beings need to learn to bear is the state of longing. Longing is a human condition. The poets speak about it. We feel it sometimes as a lack or a hunger in our souls. If we do not understand it, we think something is missing in our lives. If only we had the right job, the right partner, the right house, or the right car, our longing would go away. Our consumer life is pushed beyond this earth's capacities because we are unable to bear longing, and it seems that we are becoming less and less able to bear it. This, too, can begin in childhood. We feel dissatisfied with what we have. We want to fill the longing. Some people have it all—all the money, all the sex, all the fame—and still this longing exists. If longing is a human condition, then how can we find our right relationship to this human experience? How can we bear it in a way that supports evolution?

In "Otherwise the Darkness," Thomas Aquinas writes:

I
have a cause.
We need those don't we?
Otherwise the darkness and cold gets in
and everything starts to
ache.

My soul has a purpose, it is
to love;

if I
do not fulfill
my heart's vocation,
I suffer. [35]

The third human experience that we will go through at different times and on different levels is the desire to be accepted, along with the fear of rejection. This can be played out from the most basic need to fit in with popular culture, the latest fashions, and so on, or it can be carried into our deepest inner sanctuary with our relationship to the spiritual world. Every human being on some level has to encounter this wish to be accepted and this fear of being rejected. It is impossible to be accepted by all people all of the time.

Even though we know this and we know that it is madness to try, we still feel its effects. Even though we can rationalize it, the feeling still lives in us. How, then, can we find our right relationship to this human condition? How can we bear it?

As Hafiz says in "It Felt Love":

How
Did the rose
Ever open its heart

And give to this world
All its
Beauty?

It felt the encouragement of light
Against its
Being,

Otherwise,
We all remain

Too

Frightened. [36]

When we look at all the foolish things we have done in our life, we often find one of these three human struggles behind our actions. On the other hand, a human being who is able to bear these human experiences exudes a strong quality of maturity. A teenager who has begun to bear these human experiences will come through those most difficult years less scarred, with fewer regrets. In general, however, we do not support our children to bear these things; rather, we support them to avoid these things. We can educate them so they understand that what they are feeling and experiencing is not only a normal part of being human, but also that it is indeed essential to growth and maturity.

All human beings need to develop in growth and maturity as independent, individualized egos, for within this ego lies our freedom to choose. It is our choice to work with truth or falseness; our choice to bring beauty or ugliness into the world; our choice to do the good deed and not the immoral one. Our democratic society, built on freedom of speech and thought, should be supporting at its heart the free, independent ego. If this society is to be a part of human evolution, it must uphold the free, individualized "I."

Our greatest choice is ultimately to choose to love. No social structure, regime, or law can take away that choice; in even the most inhumane conditions that are forced upon human beings, we still have that choice. Love in the true sense is not a common bond with another. No love is perfect that proceeds from coercion, just as no good deed is really good if we chose it from fear of the consequences of doing otherwise. Love is not perfected by being linked or bound together with necessity, with unfree conditions or unconscious bonds.

Only when the ego is free and independent can it choose not to love; and only then does choosing love become a gift. Some would say this is the divine plan— to make the ego so strong and independent that it can then offer this love as an individualized gift even to the spiritual world. For this to become an individualized gift, we must learn this kind of love—love that does not arise because out of our disposition we find it satisfying to love the other; rather, we love for the other person's sake. We love for no gain for ourselves. Even if we do not agree with this, we all recognize the necessity of love for the human soul. This necessity changes not only our life on earth, but also our life in the spiritual world.

True love is a divine capacity, and therefore it can enter with us into our relationship with the spirit. We have various soul capacities that we are developing in any given incarnation. The artistic soul sees the world differently than the scientific soul does. Each capacity adds to the wholeness of the rich kingdom of life. We do not bring every capacity that is developed in one life into the next, for this may prevent developing a new capacity. Sometimes a capacity is carried, transformed, into the next life; it takes a new form, so that it will support us in our growing development. There is only one capacity that continues to develop from life to life—that grows onward and returns to grow again in each lifetime—and that is the capacity to love.

When we consider some of the pictures Steiner has shared with us of reincarnation, we can see that the path of development is not one of rising to higher and higher status in the world. In one of his very last lectures he spoke of the being John the Baptist, who in his next incarnation became the artist Raphael; and then in the incarnation after that became the poet Novalis. This is quite extraordinary to contemplate: John the Baptist, the one who baptized the Christ, is a being who is known throughout the world and lived the most significant of roles in human life. In his next life he becomes an artist who leaves the world works of art that depict spiritual reality. Many who walk the earth now know of this artist, but many others do not and would not perceive his significance. Finally, we have Novalis, who may be unknown to those who are not familiar with German culture.

Love is not a capacity that is held back, for there is no benefit to the evolving soul to leave that capacity un-incarnated; each facet becomes the soul's continual companion. We can assess the true development of individual beings only by their capacity to love. It cannot be assessed by outward status or impact on humankind, by fame or fortune, or by any other external manifestation. It can be assessed only by a capacity to love. "The mission of our Earth is the cultivation of the principle of love to its highest degree by those beings who are evolving upon it."[37] We can recognize how well we are doing with this mission, not through outer gestures alone, but through our evolving stages of development. "The higher the stage of development reached by human beings, the more the impulse of love in them increases."[38] This is our primary task, to evolve to love fully.

When students first come to this Western schooling, they feel that it is hard work. Some come from other paths of meditation, and they say the other meditation methods are like dreaming or floating compared with what is being asked in these soul-strengthening exercises. Yet as we understand the path of evolution that humanity is called upon to take and that we are on this journey together, we see why we need this strength of soul; why we need to participate in the evolution of humanity as a whole, and not separate ourselves for our own evolution.

Taking this path means that we can be more useful members of society, stronger souls capable of giving more, of doing more. We do not become subjectively hypersensitive and experience a need to close ourselves off from the world. Still, our souls are extremely sensitive to the forces existing in the world around us. Strong and sensitive beings are developed through this path. Beings capable of giving love, of giving of their very selves in service to the world.

4

INITIATION AND
THE DIVINE SPIRITUAL WORLD

E soteric pupils must first awaken the divine within themselves, awaken the higher "I." Our first recognition of this higher "I" is unlikely to be like the strong force of the astral activity; it may simply be an experience of peace. "We do not see ourselves aright if we say: 'Here am I, this robust and real man, standing upon Earth; here am I with my inmost being.' We see ourselves aright only if we say: 'Our true being is in the spiritual world, and what is here of us on earth is but a picture—an image of our true being.'"[39]

This awakening of the higher "I" is our entry into the esoteric Christmas mystery, the mystery of the conscious birth of the spirit into earthly life. It can be entered into only once the preliminary steps have been surmounted. The birth of the spirit within the soul is as transforming as the birth of a soul within the body. Our higher "I" is united with the body of love, for it is made from the same substance. Just as the little finger separated from the body does not have a life of its own, our higher "I" can never separate from that body of love. The birth of the higher "I" will be different according to the previous growth of the individual. At the beginning of our growth, the birth of the higher "I" can be compared to our consciousness as existing only in the tip of the finger of the body of love. Unlike in the past when there were the *mahatmas*, the great souls, today there is not usually a great enlightenment. In our first self-awakening, we all begin at the tip of the finger of the body of love. It is an extraordinary awakening to our true eternal self, but it is nevertheless just the beginning of this spiritual evolution. As we develop spiritually, we grow into the finger of the body of love, and we can point the way with this finger. We can beckon one person with this finger, and we can prod another. As we develop spiritually, we then grow into the hand of this body of love. We can beckon more clearly, and we can gesture and sign. It is a simple but important picture that the more we grow, the greater the effect we can have in service to the world.

In Western schooling the spiritual being that is the head of the divine spiritual world supporting humanity's progression is known as the Christ Being, the Being of Love. Unfortunately, through lifeless religion we have lost most of the esoteric knowledge of this being, of this consciousness. Like all things lost, we must regain them out of our own inner efforts. If esoteric pupils have worked not for their personal gain but with the laws of the divine spiritual world, they will eventually encounter for themselves this Being of Love. They may not know this being as the Christ Being. It may be known by many names, yet it will be recognized as the divine Being of Love. Love overcomes the separateness and division that becoming a self-aware I-being has necessarily created.

There is another force that beckons us onward toward the light of the spiritual life, and that is the Being of Light, the Being of Wisdom. We need this light, this wisdom, to shine on the way, but it should never be acquired without love.

"Spiritual Science is given to the world today because it is a necessity for humanity; but in it lies the great danger that if it is cultivated without the Christ Impulse, without the impulse of love, human beings will only increase their egotism."[40] In Anthroposophy and other Western esoteric schools we have incisive pictures that instruct us about the fact that we need to awaken our own soul activity and cultivate strong ego forces. For this reason, following gurus or enlightened ones is not seen as the path for today. It is up to us to awaken and strongly cultivate our souls and egos; but the knowledge that we have to walk the path ourselves can also block our relationship to the benevolent, supportive forces that help inner work. We must come to recognize that all the forces that presently live in us, as we are now, are not all that is required. Our gesture has to be that we are not "the be all and end all," for we do need the support of the spiritual world. There is a certain inner soul quality required to seek this support: it is a reverence and awe for something that is beyond us. We must develop reverence for those benevolent forces that lie beyond our own capacities.

Atheists, who do not believe in the spiritual world, may have very rich inner lives, with reverence and wonder for nature. There are also those scientists who have reverence and wonder for the majesty of life, even though in their scientific minds they may not believe in God or spirituality. But their reverence and wonder keep their soul life growing. Of course, there are some scientists who have no reverence or wonder, and their experience is very different. They are clinical and closed off, as opposed to the experience of someone who is openhearted and works with wonder for something that is beyond the self. To be genuine in the inner work requires that moment of coming to a place of reverence. Even before the inner work begins, reverence changes the exercises from personal maneuvers to genuine striving. Reverence is a call to spiritual beings.

Reverence and awe for the world, brought to children, are the wings required to work in the spiritual world as adults. To lay a foundation for their future inner striving, children do not need to be taught how to meditate or how to strengthen the soul life; but they do need to live in and be held in reverence. Children need to live in the presence of adults who trust in these benevolent spiritual powers, and who are striving to strengthen their own soul capacities in the bearing of human life. Once we are working with reverence for something that is beyond the self, and we have also removed ourselves (as in the sense of feeling that we are important) so that we do not block or ignore its help, we can allow the divine to help us. It stands, not as a contradiction, but as a challenge, to hold these things in the soul at the same time—to strive with inner strength of activity toward independence and at the same time to seek help from those guiding evolving beings.

It is important in our times to seek our relationship to guiding forces within our own soul. To work out of our direct inner relationship to the spirit is a sign of esoteric schooling for our times, for the esoteric schools of today must promote the next step in human development. "We need to combat the love of illusion that is so widespread today. Many feel comfortable when they can delude themselves about reality. Instead of Christ in me, who arouses my strength, who liberates powerful forces within me, they profess the Christ who is external to them, and who mercifully frees them from sins without their having to lift a finger or draw on their own forces."[41]

When first we begin an exercise, we take it on ourselves to work with it out of our own forces; because of its newness, it is not a personal habit. There can be a certain experience of grace in the new exercise, because of its newness, and the exercise can be very powerful; yet it is easy for this grace to begin to fade. The key to reigniting the exercise is reverence. If we are in a place of reverence before we say any of the verses, then we will experience the meditative verse very differently. Every time we meditate we can ask, "How do I come to it in this new way, this most living way?" The spiritual reveals itself in the present. The spirit reveals itself in the living that is found in the present. If we are just doing the exercise through memory, then we are adding more weight to our personality.

You will find that all the things you struggle with in everyday life and through your biography may even become deeply entwined in your relationship to your meditative practice. We must be vigilant and do as the Hermetic schooling suggests: watch the watcher, judge the judge, examine the examiner. This means that we must put ourselves to one side, even the tricky self. This unconscious self cannot be aware of what lies before it: "This is the secret of very many things in the spiritual world; namely that evil powers in the spiritual world can retain their power only as long as one is not aware of them."[42]

In many individuals the quality of reverence is almost like prayer. It is a gesture of realizing that we require support from the divine in the form of higher powers. Reverence is a major key if you are trying to come to the meditation in a living way. When you inwardly accept that you are not the "be all and end all," and stop forcing your practice, you are no longer fighting to do your inner work, but rather working from that gesture of reverence. From this place it is then possible to find the key to tranquility. Here you can let go of all the experiences of daily life and allow the verse to work actively on your soul forces, bearing fruit. Before we have put ourselves to one side, those maneuvers may be strengthening the everyday workaday self. When we sit to begin meditation and start from the place of recognizing why we are meditating—that this is our work, to develop our conscious relationship with the divine spiritual world—we overcome our everyday self.

All meditative practice helps not only our own development, but also the development of other beings.

"Everything that human beings do is like a summons to unknown beings."[43] The thoughts and feelings and will activity that are cultivated in relationship to the eternal divine spiritual world are like food for that world. Only thoughts that are true can penetrate through to the divine spiritual world. All other thoughts of error, selfishness, and immorality are caught in the elemental atmosphere. If we have a thought of worthlessness, this thought is not an eternal truth, but as a living force it continues to exist through feeding the beings that promote it.

Whatever we feed grows. The beings that promote eternal thoughts are fed by our inner striving. When we give all of our soul activity to a verse that is filled with eternal thoughts, it is received by those same beings. This sustenance is passed back to the earthly world to human souls. We may not receive the fruits of our meditation, but someone does. Humanity gains from our striving because once we start working with the eternal divine, we begin to work with its laws of love. The love that gives only gives. This knowledge can help us to continue onward with our inner work, knowing that humanity gains from it. The contents of the human soul are food for spiritual beings. Divine content feeds the divine beings. Egotistic content feeds egotistical beings. Materialistic content feeds materialistic beings. "If a human being has ugly, bad feelings, then these ugly, bad feelings exist around us and they attract beings who are always there waiting for these feelings. Just as physical creatures wait for food, the same applies to supersensible beings; one has only to supply them with food."[44]

The food we give through our soul activity to these various spiritual beings strengthens their capacities and therefore their power to affect the spiritual atmosphere in which we all partake. Steiner indicates that the angels need our esoteric striving and our study as food for themselves; and that the archangels utilize, to the degree esotericism penetrates us, these forces that further the development of groups of people, and for their own development.[45] Whatever work we do, we do not work for ourselves alone, even if we are trapped in this illusion. Everything that we do affects the world, and the world in turn affects us. When we look toward this manifested world, we see the inner life of previous generations around us. We can perceive the hearts of human beings who once existed on earth. We see the collective mass soul of previous generations express itself in our man-made world. We can see how much we have yet to transform; what does, and does not, reflect the divine world and its laws of love.

At some point each student of inner work will recognize that it is impossible to advance any further without the help of the higher beings, without the help of higher consciousnesses. Although it is up to our own efforts to be available for this help, we nevertheless cannot progress without other beings. "Persevere in silent inner seclusion; close the senses to all that they brought you before your training; reduce to absolute immobility all the thoughts which, according to your previous habits, surged within you; become quite still and silent within, wait in patience, and then the higher worlds will begin to fashion and perfect the organs of sight and hearing in your soul and spirit."[46]

The individual pupil advances through trials in life. Regardless of the individual's previous incarnation or stage of development, in each life the trials are presented. Having passed through these trials in a previous incarnation makes it easier to pass through them in this one. Still, it is typical to experience a trial for many years or even lifetimes before passing through it successfully for the first time. There are three primary trials on the esoteric path. They are known as the fire trial, the water trial, and the air trial. To give a picture of these trials, we can say that they begin in the full sense as exams do in any schooling. There must be many lessons and classes, much learning, and pre-exams, before the finals are taken and we pass and move onward. If we do not pass, we need to retrace our steps. If we must retrace our steps, we simply learn more, study harder, and take the test again. All previous learning has taken place in the school of life. The final exams take place once the higher "I" is born. The trials are undertaken for growth and maturation and will lead the student's soul toward greater knowledge of this higher "I."

The first is the fire trial. Like all the trials, this one takes place in life itself. Preparation for it takes place throughout our life until it culminates in an intense challenge. The fire trial has three components: we ourselves as the soul being challenged, the spiritual world that creates the challenge, and the event that is taking place in life. The trials are individual, because the blocks and the conditions that must be overcome are ours; and in their overcoming, we overcome ourselves. This is essential if we are to serve the divine spiritual world by being in service to others. It helps us develop a relationship to the spiritual world that becomes unshakeable; usually the fire trial has something of this gesture to it. It could be major illness or an external event—for example, the loss of someone close or some other strong disruption in life.

The quality we are to develop is always similar: an unshakable faith. If you are placed in the throes of this intensity, what will you do? What will you do in the intensity of the disruption to your normal life? What force in you will take hold in that moment? It is easy to sit in our comfortable lives and talk about the spiritual world; but if we receive a terminal diagnosis or undergo any major crisis, what happens then? How quickly do we lose our relationship to the spiritual world? How more intensely do we look toward it? This defining event presents some people with the opportunity, the way, to solidify their relationship to the spiritual world. For others egotism steps in and runs life. For still others materialism takes over, and they place their trust and belief in the outer appearance of things alone. We have to remember that it is not what takes place in life that determines our capacities, but how we meet what takes place in life. We are all the time being called to solidify an inexhaustible faith in the unseen. At every turn we have little trials as we are being prepared to face the final fire trial.

In daily life we forget our relationship to the unseen spiritual world, owing to the powerful forces of physical reality. Once we have passed the fire trial, we cannot forget it. We can no longer say such things as, "The doctor alone saved her life." Ultimately, we are living with the spiritual world as the greater reality. Inwardly we know that behind all external happenings the spiritual is at work. We are not paying lip service to this esoteric knowledge, but we live with it as our own knowledge. Steiner says people can go through the fire trial and have no conscious idea that they are in the midst of initiation; but afterward they will be a much greater support in others' lives. They carry something that is truly a new capacity. They hold the knowledge of meaning and purpose in life. People can pass the fire trial and not be aware that they are now working with that body of love, but they are.

If those who have passed the fire trial are conscious students of the esoteric path, they will have had the preparation to enter into the water trial. The water trial, for which we are also prepared in our life, is very different. There are only two components: the spiritual world that guides inwardly the candidate of initiation and the individual soul through whom the external expression manifests. No one can enter this trial unconsciously. All the various life experiences and meditative exercises prepare one for the water trial. When we look at the living and dying tree and experience expansion and contraction, we learn a language that is not a sense language but a soul language. When we experience the color of blue or red, we experience what blue or red does within us. We learn a nonverbal language that is spoken in the soul. In the water trial, requests are spoken into your soul, into your inner life, directly to you.

Students of the water trial are given certain tasks to perform, certain services in the world. These services are not demanded by the outer world, as with the fire trial. The instructions are given inwardly. The student has to make a commitment to perform the task that has been requested. Preparation for the trial can take place in life without our realizing it. Perhaps we find ourselves in a meeting where we must make a presentation, saying things that we find uncomfortable to say, or that we believe will not be well received. Still, we recognize it as important, and understand that it does not arise from our own personality or preferences. In such moments, we do not work out what to say in our minds. Something speaks inwardly. Something needs to be spoken, though we may not want to be the one who speaks it. This is one form of preparation for the water trial: a rightness of deed, something that needs to be said or not said, or done or not done. The soul is being prepared to serve that inner picture. Something within recognizes this inward call. It is not the personal will pushing into the world; instead, it is a willing from within. It is my free act to serve it or not.

When the water trial comes to its fullness, the student has learned this inner language more fully and receives the knowledge that is required to do particular tasks. There is no request from the external world, only from the inner world. Yet the deed takes place in the external world, and it affects the lives of others. It is the trial of service. Students cannot receive any credit for this service. They may go unseen or unrecognized completely, but they fulfill the task. The student is the bridge between the spiritual and the earthly.

The task is presented inwardly in different ways. It can sometimes be heard inwardly, but may also be experienced as an image, or as an inner activity that the student has to read correctly. In order to pass the water trial, the student has to overcome all prejudices about how the spiritual world works; about what is loving or not loving, or useful or not useful; about how the spiritual world expects human beings to behave. The student must abandon a particular expectation of what the spiritual world will give to the earthly world. All personal preferences must be overcome, as they could become our personal conditions of serving and limit our ability to serve.

We all have ideas about how the spiritual world will work for humanity, but the workings of the spiritual world are not what we think; they are beyond our range of knowledge. In all of these matters, we confront those conditions and beliefs that live within us. Everyone is being prepared for the trials. Whether a candidate succeeds in them is another matter. The student can succeed in the fire trial without knowledge of the hierarchical beings above the human being; but if the student proceeds onward and enters the water trial consciously, the student enters into the mystery of the guiding beings that are working with humanity.

Passing through this trial, the student is unable to turn back and pretend that the spiritual world does not work with humanity. When Steiner says it makes a difference which café you go to drink your coffee, it is clearly a reality for the student. When we move, the spiritual world is moving. Each one of these trials may give rise to the spiritual experience of perceiving this truth directly. The water trial leaves us with an ability to recognize and work with the guiding beings of humanity. Then I am no longer a puppet for any force that wants to maneuver things; instead, I am aligning myself with the divine, which wants humanity to evolve. I am aligning with the beings of progress. In doing so, I have to overcome all my own prejudices. The strength that the student develops in the fire trial is a necessary prerequisite to passing through the water trial. To go through the water trial without that first step would be impossible.

When the student can say, "I will absolutely carry out to the letter, unquestionably, what is asked of me by the divine spiritual world," that student has passed the water trial. In the whole preparation and process of working through the water trial, the student feels so sure of the benevolent force helping humanity that this thought becomes comfortable: "I'd like to live like this—bringing whatever needs to be brought, knowing that it is of benefit for others." However, it does not end here; the next step is presented, which is very different.

The moment the water trial is passed, another and more difficult one presents itself—one that develops a different soul capacity. It cultivates completely different faculties, but it cannot be embarked upon nor completed without the transformation acquired in the water trial. Through the proceeding trials, we have formed a continuous knowledge of the spiritual world, a spiritual world that is working with us and in the world around us. We also participate in world evolution by committing to following through with the tasks of the spirit. What all the trials have in common is that they strengthen the relationship to the body of love.

The air trial is much harder than the preceding two. There is no spiritual world giving direction. There are no Masters of Wisdom and Harmony guiding us. There is only the direct relationship to the higher "I." The student is being called upon by the one and only component of the air trial, the higher "I." In passing the air trial, anything that stands in the way of a direct relationship to the higher "I" has to be overcome. It requires total presence of mind. The student knows by this time what the difference is between the higher presence and the other, everyday self. During the previous trials, growth of the higher "I" has occurred. The main struggle the student has at this point is to be completely still in soul and, at the same time, connected to the spiritual world, in order that the higher "I" can speak and be heard in the noise and dynamics of life.

This trial is prepared for in life when an event occurs and the response needs to be immediate. There is no time to waste. There is no time to weigh it. You cannot do the Y exercise. Using the Y symbol is a preparation to gain a sense of the active quality of the higher "I," but the trials take place in life itself, not in meditative practice.

The air trial requires an instantaneous recognition of what is required, and must be immediately acted upon. In this trial the student alone affects the outcome of the situation. If you do not act in the moment, the response called for by the opportunity is gone, and gone for good. If the student does not perform the given task in the water trial, in some way it will still be fulfilled. On the other hand, in the air trial the task is left and remains undone if the student does not perform the perceived task. The undoneness resounds within. The opportunity does not return. The experience is similar to that which surrounds some deaths, in knowing that something that could have been accomplished before that final moment, has now been left undone. More opportunities to pass the air trial will present themselves if the student is willing to work onward; but they will be quite different and more demanding, until finally the student recognizes all the aspects and blocks of this trial. In completion of this trial, the student affirms the relationship to the body of love and becomes an active member of that united force for the good.

In studying these trials, we recognize the three main gestures of human evolution: the overcoming of materialism, amplified and tested in the fire trial; the overcoming of egotism, which challenges us in the water trial; and the development of our relationship to the higher "I," put to the greatest test in the air trial. They are really complete only when we see how they work together. No one having passed the third trial could consider the human being as a slave of the spirit. The third trial puts our spiritual role as a participant in life in the right context. "Those who would comprehend the voice of the spirit without, they have first to experience their own spiritual self."[47] Before we pass each of these trials in everyday life, we are being prepared for them. Not a day goes by without presenting us with the possibility of strengthening our souls in these three directions: as strength in the realization of the spirit in the face of difficulties; as an inner sense for and recognition of humanity's divine helpers; and as a willingness to stand active in the present moment in our higher "I."

The trials passed give a sense of solidity, a certainty that cannot be taken away. We no longer need to remind ourselves of the existence of spiritual beings. We no longer need to remind ourselves of the human being's evolution. We no longer need to remind ourselves of who we are and why we are here. Of course, we still dwell in our external self, but at the same time we become fully conscious of our inner spiritual power.

When acting out of this higher spiritual power, we act out of the body of love. "When we act out of our own self, we are then conscious of acting also out of the eternal being of things, because the things give utterance in us in their being. We, therefore, act in harmony with the eternal world order when we direct our actions out of the eternal living within us."[48] In the contemplation of the trials we can find the gifts of the schooling exercises, which, along with life, have prepared the student to ready themselves for these trials and make their passing all the more possible.

The Guardians of the Threshold

It is possible, though not beneficial, to cross the threshold to the spiritual world without encountering the Lesser Guardian.[49] All students of the path will hope to encounter this Lesser Guardian, for it is a sign that they are walking the true path. This meeting also ensures that what is experienced does not come from within us, as all that comes from the personal self now appears to the student's view in the form of the Lesser Guardian. The preparation required to encounter the Lesser Guardian makes us able to stand aside from our individual capacities of thinking, feeling, and willing. It is our own higher "I," clothed in all the forms that live in us from this life and from all our previous lives that merge to make this one being that stands before us now as the Lesser Guardian.

These forms that merge into one and clothe the higher "I" live in both true and false thinking; in both beautiful and ugly feelings; and in both good and immoral intentions and deeds. If the student has not walked the path of purification and preparation, and has not been able to stand aside from the personal, workaday self, it is possible through certain techniques and keys to pass the threshold without this encounter. This is not helpful in the training of our times, and therefore not given in the true esoteric schools. If these techniques are used, the student may not have strengthened the soul in the evolutionary sense, but now returns to a relationship with the spiritual world without any independent activity. The drop returns to the ocean and not only loses itself, but has no awareness that this is so.

This is a weakened soul state. This is a return to how it was for the human being in a past evolutionary stage—before the individual higher "I" could become a fifth sheath of the human being; before the higher "I" sheath came into individual activity as a new element of self-development. Without this soul strength, our experience of the spiritual world is limited. Without this higher "I," our experience of the ocean of the spirit obliterates individual awareness. In the new paradigm, the drop returns to the ocean but stays in and aware of itself.

The experience of the spiritual world and the duration of our stay there are dependent on our capacities. These capacities allow the student to receive what exists in the spiritual world. If there is little capacity and we cross into the spiritual world, we may find it a world of little substance. All depends on what we bring with us. We light the way of the spiritual world ourselves. If we have little fuel, we may light only a small space. The fuel is gained from the overcoming of hindrances and the development of free soul capacities. The lamp itself is gained through the birth of the higher "I." This higher "I" is born from the forces gained from the independent, individualized, free ego that surrenders its forces for the coming into being of the higher "I."

The individual capacities that each student takes into the spiritual world change the type and depth of experience that is possible in these various realms. Each of the seven realms of the true spiritual world has several stages of development that are passed through by the evolving being; only some of these can be described here. One individual may cross into the spiritual world into the moon sphere on the first level, and there will experience consciousness outside of the body. To all that the student perceives of trees, land, water, and so on, the consciousness will be able to say "I am that." There is no difference between the rock and the body; the consciousness can say "I am that" to both equally, with no preference. Another individual may cross the threshold into the moon sphere on a higher level of perception; he will perceive the sun and say of this sun, "my heart."

Beginner candidates of initiation most commonly pass through the first level of each sphere. In the second sphere, and the second crossing into the spiritual world, we are shown the workings of the great beings that influence humanity's development. They are sometimes referred to as the Masters of Wisdom and Harmony. They are the great initiates working from the spiritual world, as well as purely spiritual beings who support the progression of humanity. All these beings are involved in the weaving of lives and the events that unfold in the external world.

The third crossing reveals another spiritual truth. Here we perceive how every individual human being is creating the collective atmosphere that affects the destiny of the whole world. Here it is made evident that our thoughts and feelings continue to have an impact on that collective atmosphere. Humanity's future karma is revealed. Every detail of our individual biography (the events of our life) takes its impulse from this collective atmosphere. The student is initiated into the laws of karma from the individual to humanity as a whole. The fourth crossing leads us to the Sun sphere and potentially to the Greater Guardian.

What happens to the spiritual truths that reveal themselves to the human soul that crosses the threshold in these different spheres? It is dependent on our preparation, on what lives in the soul before the experience of crossing this threshold. How will we be able to integrate and live with the reality of what we now know? For those unprepared, the first crossing to the moon sphere could leave them feeling that life is just an illusion, that they have been caught in maya, living a lie. They can end up feeling despondent and unable to continue as a useful member of society. For those who cross unprepared into the second sphere, it can leave them with the feeling that they are puppets, that nothing they do really matters, and that there is no free will. This can leave the soul incapacitated in relation to earthly life, or even destructive toward others. If seekers cross the threshold unprepared and enter the third sphere, they may feel that they just want to leave this world, escape the wheel of life and death. They may see that if they clear up their personal karma, they can escape the karmic cycle of dying and returning to earth. This may then lead to a life of working simply to liberate the individual self.

All prepared crossings into this realm of the spiritual world require an encounter with the Lesser Guardian each time; the crossing and meeting do not constitute a one-time encounter, although each encounter can certainly change its expression. For the prepared soul, each crossing into the temple of wisdom benefits not only the student but also the surrounding world. Students become advocates for human evolution. They are compassionate to those who have been waylaid on the path. They know that the true path has to be walked by each individual alone. They give their lives to encourage this journey.

The Greater Guardian is not encountered fully until the threshold of the Sun sphere.[50] Here the higher "I," which has continued to grow in the body of love, reveals for a brief moment in time what human beings will become if they continue on this evolutionary path. The higher "I" now grows together fully with the Being of Love. The Christ Being grows together with the higher "I," showing the future potential of humanity. This Greater Guardian experience shows us the ideal for which we strive. The Christ shows himself as the great ideal of humankind on earth.

Without the proper preparation, this future perception may leave us with an illusion of progress. We may think that we are already this evolved higher "I" and not recognize it as the future toward which we must energetically work. The Lesser Guardian experience can safeguard us from this illusion. Prepared students hold these two experiences side by side: what they are and what they are to become.

If we were to reach the sun's sphere without preparation, and encounter the spiritually illuminated being, the bearer of light and wisdom, it would be hard to resist the temptation, which comes in this moment, to stay in the spiritual world. The Sun Being we encounter is once again determined by the preparation of the soul. If we do not know the Being of Love within us, then that place will be empty, and we will encounter just the Being of Light. The prepared soul is able to receive the task set by the Greater Guardian—that the student's newborn self has to direct and lead the ordinary self. "Man beholds his newborn self as another being standing before him, but he cannot perceive it completely. For whatever stage he may have reached upon the way into the supersensible worlds, there are always still higher stages. At these stages he will perceive ever more and more of his 'higher self.' This 'higher self' can thus only partially reveal itself to the student of the spiritual at any of these stages."[51]

We cannot serve two masters at the same time; either the lower ego or the higher ego will have supremacy. It is up to each individual to determine this. The battle is fought between all that we are and all that we can become, all that we will be. It is staged between the past self and the future self. The newborn self is strengthened when we refuse to allow this "double" of the past to act against the interests of the newborn self. Each new hindrance we overcome will produce new capacities for the next step of development.

Once this newborn self is liberated from the battle of overcoming the personal double, which has been revealed by the Lesser Guardian, it then sets out upon the long journey of liberating the forces in the outer human being. In the speech of the deity to warriors in the Bhagavad Gita: "Do fight: whom I have killed, do you kill." All have to pass through this stage. This is where the great work really begins, even though we may imagine this to be the destination. This new and arduous task will eventually lead the human being through the Sun sphere, where the Being of Love and the Being of Light unite to guide the way. It is in the Sun sphere that we enter into the esoteric Easter mysteries. This is not the birth of the higher "I" of the Christmas mysteries, but what follows this birth. In its highest form it is the transubstantiation, death, and resurrection.

The Easter mysteries are the hardest of all ordeals, and cannot be understood or entered into until all previous trials and tests have been endured. The story of the Christian year portrays the story of the spiritual path that all initiates walk. Until we endure winter, we cannot welcome the spring of renewal. This image is not of the outer seasons but of the inner seasons. We become familiar with our inner yearly cycle even as we celebrate the collective cycle of the outer world.

On the meditative path, human beings gain the strength to prevent the outer self from dominating the inner self. By our own efforts, we bring out of ourselves liberated soul forces that allow the higher "I" to come to active being. The higher "I" then works to transform the sheaths of the outer body so that they will surrender their forces to become the vehicle for the higher "I" to live fully in the spiritual world. This is the transubstantiation that takes place after death. It is here that the Rosicrucian meditation becomes a living reality:

Ex Deo nascimur
(From God we are born);
In Christo morimur
(In Christ we die);
Per Spiritum sanctum reviviscimus
(We are resurrected through the Holy Spirit).

The first transubstantiation is of the astral body, which develops the sheath known as the Spirit-Self, or Manas—the spiritual sheath for the individualized higher "I" being.[52] Through this transforming of the astral body, the "I" will have an individualized spiritual body in the cosmic ocean of the spiritual world. At the same time, penetration and transformation of the etheric body are occurring, but at a much slower rate. The transformation of the etheric body gives the substance required to develop the Life-Spirit, or Buddhi, which allows the "I" being to live entirely as a conscious spiritual being. Finally, the higher "I" liberates the forces of the physical body that become the Spirit-Man, or Atma.

The great initiates have walked this path; they have transformed their outer selves, and in doing so have transformed the outer world. They face far greater battles than their own egotism. They face the forces that create the things that attack humankind in unseen warfare at all levels of their being. The initiates work tirelessly to affect the spiritual atmosphere through transforming and transmuting the diverting forces that blind humanity. Living this path is required to not fear evil but to transform it. It is the only way to gain the strength that combats these adversaries and the love that transforms them.

We have to begin where we are now. It is the only place to begin. This path has so many steps, and we would be overwhelmed if we looked in detail at all the steps in front of us. Yet it is always helpful to know the direction we are headed. To the beginner candidate for initiation, the fruits may seem far away, and yet it is tangible. Through the cycle of the spiritual year, we participate in these spiritual mysteries. Each year provides a possibility to take another step on this extraordinary path. If we survey the path we have trodden thus far, we will see that all steps cycle around to a deeper level, and that the step we stand on now has its reflection in both higher and lower stages of the path.

We will recognize that, in fact, all human beings on this path are walking together; as the ones before us on the path of initiation step up, they make the way clearer for us. As we step up, we make the way clearer for others. The well-trodden path has clearer tracks because of others. We need each other's striving. Every one of us has the capacity to work onward; and all that is asked of us—all that is ever asked of us—is to take our next step.

Notes

The quotations from Rudolf Steiner's works cited in the text have been edited to reflect gender-inclusive language.

With grateful acknowledgment to Daniel Ladinsky for the use of excerpts from his poetry translations as noted below.

1. Rudolf Steiner, *Macrocosm and Microcosm* (London: Rudolf Steiner Press 1985)

2. Steiner, *Macrocosm and Microcosm.*

3. Steiner, *How to Know Higher Worlds: A Modern Path of Initiation.* Translated by Christopher Bamford. Foreword by Arthur Zajonc. (Hudson, NY: Anthroposophic Press, 1994). The earlier edition of this book is: *Knowledge of the Higher Worlds. How Is It Achieved?* 6th revised edition. Translated by D.S. Osmond and C. Davy. (London: Rudolf Steiner Press 1969; Forest Row, Sussex, UK: Rudolf Steiner Press, facsimile reprint 2004).

4. Steiner, *Theosophy: An Introduction to the Spiritual Processes in Human Life and in the Cosmos* (Hudson, NY: Anthroposophic Press 1994).

5. Mabel Collins, *Light on the Path* (London: George Redway, 1888, reprinted by Theosophical University Press, Pasadena, CA).

6. Daniel Ladinsky, trans., *Love Poems from God: Twelve Sacred Voices from the East and West* (New York: Penguin Group 2002).

7. Steiner, *Understanding Healing. Meditative Reflections on Deepening Medicine through Spiritual Science* (Forest Row, Sussex, UK: Rudolf Steiner Press 2013). Also published as *Course for Young Doctors* (Chestnut Ridge, NY: Mercury Press).

8. Ladinsky, trans., *Love Poems*.

9. Steiner, *How to Know Higher Worlds*.

10. Rabindranath Tagore, "Stray Birds," trans. R. Tagore (NY: Macmillan Company 1916).

11. Steiner, *Guidance in Esoteric Training* (Forest Row, Sussex, UK: Rudolf Steiner Press 1999).

12. Steiner, *The World of the Senses and the World of the Spirit* (London: Rudolf Steiner Press 1979).

13. Steiner, *Theosophy*.

14. Steiner, *Guidance in Esoteric Training*.

15. Steiner, *An Outline of Esoteric Science* (Hudson, NY: Anthroposophic Press 1997).

16. Steiner, in *Start Now! A Book of Soul and Spiritual Exercises*, ed. Chris Bamford (Great Barrington, MA: SteinerBooks 2004).

17. Steiner, in *Start Now! A Book of Soul and Spiritual Exercises*.

18. Ladinsky trans., *Love Poems*.

19. *Secret Symbols of the Rosicrucians of the 16th and 17th Centuries* (San Jose, CA: AMORC 1987).

20. Steiner, *How to Know Higher Worlds*.

21. Steiner, *A Way of Self-Knowledge: And the Threshold of the Spiritual World* (Great Barrington, MA: Anthroposophic Press 2006).

22. Steiner, *The Christian Mystery: Early Lectures* (Great Barrington, MA: Anthroposophic Press 1998).

23. Steiner, *Esoteric Science*.

24. Steiner, *How to Know Higher Worlds*.

25. Ladinsky, trans., *I Heard God Laughing: Poems of Love and Joy by Hafiz* (NY: Penguin Group 2006).

26. Steiner, *The Apocalypse of St. John* (Great Barrington, MA: Anthroposophic Press 1993).

27. Ladinsky, trans., *I Heard God Laughing.*

28. Steiner, *Theosophy.*

29. Steiner, *Esoteric Lessons, vol. 1, 1904-1909; vol. 2, 1910-1912; vol. 3 1913-1923* (Great Barrington, MA: Anthroposophic Press 2006; 2013; 2011).

30. Steiner, *Secrets of the Threshold* (Hudson, NY: Anthroposophic Press 1987).

31. Steiner, *Goethe's Standard of the Soul, as Illustrated in* Faust *and in the Fairy Story of "The Green Snake and the Beautiful Lily"* (Anthroposophical Publishing, 1925).

32. Steiner, *Spiritual Hierarchies and the Physical World: Zodiac, Planets, and Cosmos* (Great Barrington, MA: SteinerBooks 2008).

33. Ladinsky, trans., *I Heard God Laughing.*

34. Ladinsky, trans., *The Subject Tonight Is Love: 60 Wild and Sweet Poems of Hafiz* (NY: Penguin Compass 2003).

35. Ladinsky, trans., *Love Poems.*

36. Ladinsky, trans., *The Gift: Poems by Hafiz* (NY: Penguin Compass 1999).

37. Steiner, *The Gospel of St. John* (Spring Valley, NY: Anthroposophic Press, 1962).

38. Steiner, *Love and Its Meaning in the World* (Great Barrington, MA: Anthroposophic Press, 1998).

39. Steiner, *Man as a Picture of the Living Spirit* (Forest Row, Sussex, UK: Rudolf Steiner Press, 1972).

40. Steiner, *Man as a Picture of the Living Spirit.*

41. Steiner, *Whitsun and Ascension: An Introductory Reader* (Forest Row, Sussex, UK: Rudolf Steiner Press, 2007).

42. Steiner, Lecture, Dornach, September 21, 1923.

43. Steiner, *The Influence of the Spiritual Beings upon Man* (Spring Valley, NY: 1982).

44. Steiner, Lecture, Berlin June 1, 1908.

45. Steiner, *Esoteric Lessons, vol. 3.*

46. Steiner, *How to Know Higher Worlds.*

47. Steiner, *Esoteric Lessons, vol. 1.*

48. Steiner, *Theosophy.*

49. Steiner, *Esoteric Science.*

50. Steiner, *Esoteric Science.*

51. Steiner, *Esoteric Science.*

52. Steiner, *Theosophy.*

LISA ROMERO is the author of several books on inner development, as well as a complementary health practitioner and an adult educator who has been offering healthcare and education enriched by anthroposophy since 1993. From 2006, the primary focus of her work has been on teaching inner development and anthroposophic meditation.

Her six books are *The Inner Work Path: A Foundation for Meditative Practice in the Light of Anthroposophy* (2014); *Developing the Self – Through the Inner Work Path in the Light of Anthroposophy* (2015); *Living Inner Development: The Necessity of True Inner Development in the Light of Anthroposophy* (2016); *Sex Education and the Spirit: Understanding Our Communal Responsibility for the Healthy Development of Gender and Sexuality within Society* (2017); *Spirit-led Community: Healing the Impact of Technology* (2018); and *A Bridge to Spirit: Understanding Conscious Self Development and Consciousness-Altering Substances* (2019).

Through the Inner Work Path, Lisa offers lectures, courses, and retreats for personal and professional development in communities and schools worldwide. Lisa's capacity to deliver esoteric wisdom with insight and understanding allows her to meet the diverse needs of communities and professions.

For many years, Lisa lectured on health and nutrition and male/female studies at Sydney Rudolf Steiner College, where she continues to give lectures on inner development to the tutors.

Since 1999, she has been presenting on the subject of gender, sexuality, and spiritual life. She has been working with Waldorf schools as a part of their "health and wellbeing" curriculum, working directly with the students, teachers, and parents on this theme. Lisa has contributed to and is an adviser for the "Health and Personal Development for the Australian Steiner Curriculum Framework." She has developed training courses and facilitates professional development on this subject for teachers and health professionals.

Lisa designed and facilitated EduCareDo "Towards Health and Healing," which has offered eight-year courses focused on working with therapists from all modalities, as well as with Waldorf teachers toward cultivating the depth of anthroposophic insight through practical applications of therapeutic and pedagogical methods.

Lisa Romero is a tutor, contributor, and director of Inner Work Path, EduCareDo, Developing the Self – Developing the World, and the Y Project. EduCareDo offers self-directed, distance-learning courses based on the principal ideas of Rudolf Steiner. Developing the Self – Developing the World offers community education, and the Y Project supports the transition of young people into healthy community life.

For meditation courses and talks,
visit innerworkpath.com

For more information on school and community education,
visit developingtheself.org

For distance learning courses in anthroposophy,
visit educaredo.org

CPSIA information can be obtained
at www.ICGtesting.com
Printed in the USA
BVHW031407100222
628586BV00003B/454

9 780648 490425